Red Snow Fence

Also by Harry E. Northup

Books

- *Amarillo Born*
- *the jon voight poems*
- *Eros Ash*
- *Enough the Great Running Chapel*
- *the images we possess kill the capturing*
- *The Ragged Vertical*
- *Reunions*
- *Greatest Hits: 1966–2001*

Audio

- *Personal Crime*
- *Homes*

Red Snow Fence

Poems

Harry E. Northup

11-26-06
TO TERENCE WINCH,
BEST WISHES,
Harry E. Northup

Acknowledgments

Some of these poems originally appeared in

Chiron Review
ARTLIFE
SOLO

Thanks to Liz and Rick Berman.

Cover photos:	Larry Nelson
Cover design:	Robert Walker
Typesetting / book design:	Jordan Jones

Printed in the United States of America by McNaughton & Gunn, Inc. Saline, MI

ISBN-10 0-9715519-5-2
ISBN-13 978-0-9715519-5-4
Library of Congress Control Number 2005910714

First Edition / Cahuenga Press / www.cahuengapress.com

Cahuenga Press is owned, financed and operated by its poet-members James Cushing, Phoebe MacAdams, Harry E. Northup, and Holly Prado Northup. Our common goal is to create fine books of poetry by poets whose work we admire and respect; to make poetry actual in the world in ways which honor both individual creative freedom and cooperative support.

Cahuenga Press
1256 N. Mariposa Ave.
Los Angeles, CA 90029

Contents

The Night Has Always Been A Friend 7-20-03 to 11-26-03

Red Snow Fence 12-31-03 to 7-27-04

Actualities

The Reason Heart

Red Snow Fence

Everyday Things

Recluse 4-12-05 to 9-27-05

For Holly Prado Northup

& Dylan Northup

In memory of George & Marie Northup

Red Snow Fence

(A Long Poem in Time
Composed from 10-5-02
to 7-27-04)

Grave Markers

10-5-02 to 2-5-03

jobs

delivered the *rocky mountain news*
21 daily, 95 sunday, 6th grade

delivered the *scottsbluff star herald*
8th grade

thinned beets, picked tomatoes
laid on my back, put asbestos on pipes
under hospital walkways

sold clothes at dalton's men's shop, age 15
sold clothes at greenlee's, age 16

worked as a secretary & dj at ksid

united states navy, boot camp, 3 months
imperial beach: swept, swabbed, waxed,
buffed tunnel for 3 months, radio
school 6 months, radioman stationed
at pearl harbor & wahiawa 2 years
age 17 yrs 10 mos. to 20 yrs 11 mos.
(worked 3 days mess duty treasure is-
land, age 18)

cafeteria worker, briefly, age 21

briefly worked as a laborer on a grain
elevator

apprentice, summer stock, building flats,
painting, gathering props, putting up
& tearing down sets, acting, age 21

messenger, quicksilver messenger service,
41st st, off fifth avenue, age 22, first
job in new york city

summer stock, age 22, 2nd year lake
whalom playhouse, fitchburg, mass.

clerk typist, stock boy — men's suits, slacks,
waiter, counterman, nyc, 1963–1968
worked longest at simple simon hamburger
bar, 14th & 7th, 14th between seventh &
eighth — 3 hours supper & all day saturday;
"downtown," waiter, fri., sat. & sun. nights
8 p.m. to 1, 2 a.m., made $35 a night, lived
at 25th & tenth, 3 ½ rms, 5 floor walk-up,
$53 a month, 1 year

played a mental patient in the movie
"lilith," got my s.a.g. card

played the rapist in scorsese's "who's
that knocking at my door?" 1 day's
work as an actor, my first real part
in a movie, the first of 6 straight
films i worked in for scorsese

worked as a waiter at the friar's club,
55 e. 55th st, for 3 months when i
first got married

waiter at neil's, 63rd & third, day
waiter at maxwell's plum, night

i lived in nyc from 1963–1968 & studied
acting for 5 years with frank corsaro
married rita solomon oct. 31, 1967, nyc

moved to l.a., arrived march 5, 1968
got an apartment 10th & california,
santa monica &
got a waiter's job at the old world
restaurant on the strip that day
worked there two years

played a prison guard in "judd for
the defense," my first tv job, age 28

in 1970, i got the part of parker in
"the all-american boy," worked 2
months in san francisco & vacaville,
made enough money for myself, wife
& son to live on for a year

acted in "high chaparral," 2 "alias
smith & jones," (tv series)

worked as a janitor at nyberg's dry
cleaners late afternoons & saturdays
for a few months

went to santa monica college & c.s.u.n.
on the g.i. bill late '60s & early '70s

played harvey hall, deputy sheriff
in "boxcar bertha"

was jerry (vietnam vet) in "mean streets"
separated from rita northup
worked as a waiter on weekends for a few
months at pat collins, the hip hypnotist,
on the strip

played joe & jim's bartender in "alice
doesn't live here anymore"

drove a cab for santa monica red
top for 10 months in 1974 & 1975
while going to college at c.s.u.n.
my last straight job
got a part in jaglom's "tracks" in
april, 1975, quit driving a cab
played an fbi agent in "crazy mama"
for the first of 9 acting jobs for
jonathan demme
played doughboy in "taxi driver,"
for scorsese in n.y.c., age 34
did 9 films in 2 years
continued to work as an actor in
36 films, 41 tv shows, 5 commercials
through 2002
last worked as an actor in feb. & march,
played supreme court justice fitz-
simmons in abc's "the court," co-starring,
recurring role, acted in 5 out of 6
shows

last sat. night, i got $100 for reading
my poetry at the carnegie art museum,
oxnard, ca., on oct. 11, i get $200

to read my poetry at the ojai library
i have given many poetry readings
over the years

i am 62
when i hit 60, i began collecting my
s.a.g. pension: $814 a month
i continue to receive residuals
when i hit 65, i'll get social security

when i was young, i set pins in the
s.o.d. bowling alley, 6¢ a line

10 5 02

the white forehead

the mark of a good man is his honesty
the elevation of his heart is in his
compassion
many poets i know seek money & power
many are materialists
many are narrow & are abstract
many have no sense of reality
academics, administrators follow thee
home to bind, gather, to give
to be human
a poet is a practical man
he has eyes to see for himself
he lives among men, women, animals,
angels
he does not live among one
he learns from men, women & the para-
bles of past erudite thinkers
he worships a real god who cares
for all
he has a word
he gives & keeps
he lives up to his word
he lives in a real world of people
he does not limit himself to one
sex or one mathematical mind
he assumes breath

10 9 02

family & new york

yesterday, i watched a 60 minute documentary on scorsese. opening clips of "mean streets" were shown & my name appeared. "mean streets" has always been important to me not only because it's an original film — my favorite scorsese film, it's like a small jewel — but because something inside me was dislodged — a psychic dislodgement because of the emotion & violence in my scene & it opened things up for me as an actor & a poet.
scorsese talked about honesty & dignity being important in his growing up — in his family.
he also talked about seeing "on the waterfront" & liking the reality & honesty in the acting & how in "mean streets," "taxi driver," "raging bull" & "goodfellas," there was honesty & a reality in the acting & a real spirituality about who these people are.
i learned a similar thing about acting when i studied acting with frank corsaro 1963–1968 in n.y.c. & i feel the same thing about my acting in scorsese's films: "who's that knocking at my door?" "boxcar bertha," "mean streets," "alice doesn't live here anymore," "taxi driver," & "new york, new york," & his first tv show, an "amazing stories" entitled "mirror, mirror" &
i feel the same way about my poetry which has a base in the acting foundation learned in corsaro's workshop & in my early spiritual relationship with lee hickman concerning poetry. honesty & realism in a real spiritual way. with a sense of fidelity to the word. such that if a man gives his word, he lives up to his word. not a bad way to live one's life.

books

i am presently reading *jack kerouac,*
by tom clark (thunder's mouth press),
& *martin luther king, jr.,* by marshall
frady (penguin lives). other penguin
lives' biographies that i have read
in the last few years:
larry mcmurtry on *crazy horse;*
edmund white on *marcel proust;*
peter gay on *mozart;*
garry wills on *saint augustine;*
jonathan spence on *mao zedong;*
*edna o'brien on *james joyce;*
elizabeth hardwick on *woodrow wilson;*
sherwin nuland on *leonardo da vinci;*
nigel nicolson on *virginia woolf;*
*carol shields on *jane austen;*
karen armstrong on the *buddha;*
r.w.b. lewis on *dante;*
francine du plessix gray on *simone weil;*
patricia bosworth on *marlon brando;*
wayne koestenbaum on *andy warhol;*
paul johnson on *napoleon;*
*jane smiley on *charles dickens.*

(*my favorites.)

10 10 02

friday in ojai

holly & i drove to ojai
we arrived at judy & ren's at 4:45 p.m.
phoebe was there
we relaxed & talked for 45 minutes
changed clothes, went to eat
i had grilled salmon, mashed potatoes
& spinach
after supper, we drove a short way
to the ojai library

a good-sized crowd
judy introduced phoebe
phoebe read poems from her new manuscript,
livelihood, which cahuenga press
will publish next
poems about teaching
she also read poems about her home &
husband & flowers & camping out
a deep clear resonant sound

i read second: poems from *reunions*
themes: place — east hollywood; work —
summer stock, lake whalom playhouse,
fitchburg, mass.; love & care for holly;
poetics — "the study"
a very good reading — warm audience response

holly closed the reading
with poems from *specific mysteries,*
esperanza: . . . , & 2 poems for me
depth & mystery & excellent use of
language

we each made $200
& sold $132 worth of books
i sold 5 *reunions*
people were kind & praising afterward
a warm, relaxed feeling

coffee & cookies were provided
by stir crazy

the librarian told me she was touched
by my poetry about my 25-year re-
lationship with holly, its love

we went back to judy & ren's
where a dozen people gathered
to talk

at 11, i climbed into a cool bed

10 14 02

demme invited us to a world premiere

last evening at 5
holly & i ate at kate mantilini's
she had a glass of white wine
& a garden burger
i ate a meat loaf sandwich

at 6:45, we picked up our tickets
at will call at the academy
for the world premiere of
demme's "the truth about charlie"
we walked back over the red carpet
past the photographers
& went in, up the stairs
& got good seats on the aisle
left side, about ⅔rds up from the screen

i said hello to the producers, edward saxon
& neda, the cinematographer, tak
fujimoto, evelyn purcell, film director &
demme's ex-wife, mary, demme's assistant,
tracey walter & charles napier, actors,
pablo ferro, who did the titles, joe
viola, film producer/director — i introduced
all to holly — some she knew
all have worked with demme, like
i have, over many years

we enjoyed the movie — a remake
of "charade"
a joyful & exciting & elegant &
imaginative film
strikingly beautiful & loving

after the film, we went downstairs
to the reception
i ate 4 large, fresh shrimp
with cocktail sauce
& a small napoleon & a small
chocolate eclair with a cup
of decaf

then holly & i walked around the
lobby — we talked to roger corman
& met film director curtis harring-
ton
we talked with pat, ed's mother
we said hello to jonathan at the
foot of the stairs
"stunning, bright & dark thriller,"
i said
holly complimented him on the
racial mix
"was the hotel langlois an homage
to langlois?" i asked
"you have a good eye for details,"
jonathan said. "he created the
cinematheque in paris."
"which was anna karina?"
"the gypsy singer"
"was that a photo of langlois at the
stamp place?"
"no, that was kenny utt"

we thanked jonathan & went out
to wilshire
walked to doheny
north a block
got in our car & drove home
i felt clean & uplifted
"jonathan is a genuinely nice person,"
holly said

10 17 02

2

this evening & tonight
i saw myself in "mean streets"
& "the silence of the lambs"
two great films, two great directors

at a reunion for people who worked
on "beloved," at the chateau marmont,
bungalow 4
i asked demme, "who's your favorite
director?"
"scorsese," he said
"no, i mean . . . of the old timers"
"i'll have to think about that"

they are both great with actors

10 19 02

his first six

as much as i love
working with demme & kaplan
i will never get over
not working with scorsese

the first time i met him
in a 42nd street office
we connected
the first time i worked for him
in his first feature
i knew he was a born filmmaker
each successive film erupted
in me a sense of violence, humility,
kindness, joy, fun, camaraderie
he loves actors
he's a student & master of film
of light, color, movement, music

he's a film historian & preserver
he hired me to act in his first
6 features & first tv show
i will always be grateful

10 22 02

studio at night

tonight i went to raleigh studios
to see "the quiet american," based
on the graham greene novel, directed
by philip noyce, & starring michael
caine
a good story, love & war, woman as
metaphor for country — vietnam
with cia involvement
a british correspondent
set in early '50s when france
was fighting

a good film
somewhat arbitrary ending
caine's always good

noyce examines the beginning
of america's involvement
intertwined with rivals in love

walking through the lot
past trucks, star waggons, actors,
director & crew
brought back memories when i
acted in 5 shows of "the court"
earlier this year

11 5 02

"How does it feel to be a working actor?"

An actor goes through a lot with his nerves. Sometimes I think being an actor is a test of nerves. You don't work for a while & then you "have to get it out, get it up & get it in" on command. In public. I liken it to being a hit man. You lie on your bed in a hotel for lengths of time & then you get your call & you have to deliver. And it's a very competitive business. And so much depends on each time out.

When you get a job, you do your preparation: learn lines, study the script, observe humanity for creation of your character, make physical, emotional, verbal, visual choices — leaving room for new things that may come along.

When working, relaxation & concentration are primary.

I always get hyped up the night before, but once I am in costume & makeup, I feel more composed. Always a little edge, though.

Two weeks ago, after the doctor for the insurance company said my blood pressure was acceptable for me to be insured to work on 5 of the 6 shows of "The Court" that ABC bought, a fellow actor said, "You never looked so calm." I replied, "That's because I was accepted."

3 5 02

critics, brit film director, film

we are blessed to have 3 first
rate film critics who write for
the *l.a. times:* turan, dargis,
thomas.

last night, holly & i ate at the
red lobster, wilshire & la cienega.
i had a 2 lb. maine lobster, french
fries & a caesar salad, & a bud light.
she had a lobster & scallop dish,
with mixed vegetables, caesar
salad & 2 glasses of white wine.
an excellent meal.

then we went to the academy
to see mike leigh's "all or no-
thing." deep sorrow, rage, pover-
ty, struggle among the working
class in england. very moving
picture. emotional & still. the
father, mother, daughter & a neigh-
bor who irons for a living & has
a fine singing voice are all
real. a quite brilliant film.

11 10 02

nov. 12, 2002

today is my mother's birthday
she was born in kansas in 1902

she was loving & gentle, hard working
she gave birth to 4 boys & 1 girl
she died in 1970

dorothy marie monk
i never saw her throw her arms
around another man
she was devoted to her husband

when i went to be an apprentice
in summer stock, 1962, she saw
me off on the train, gave me
$20 a week for food

in 1962, i played billie brown in
eugene o'neill's "the great god
brown" at college
mother took the train 225
miles to kearney to see me act
she stayed overnight in a hotel

i never heard her say a swear word
she blushed in her 60s, when daddy
told an off-color joke

mother always put her family ahead
of herself
she let her teeth go

she had many flower-print dresses
in the closet
she was the postmistress at s.o.d.
for 12 years
she drove 12 miles in rain, sleet &
snow to get to work
she never missed a day

when she came home
she cooked & ironed

“me so tired,” she used to say
“i feel like i’ve been wrung
through a wringer”

kansas to sidney
with many towns in between

11 12 02

time passeth all understanding

when i was 17
i joined the navy on a kitty cruise
got out the day before i was 21

when i was 22
i quit college
went to new york, auditioned for summer stock
did summer stock, got my equity card

when i was 26
i acted in scorsese's first feature film

when i was 28
my son dylan was born

the ages & the films are numerous
my father died in '67 & my mother died in '70

when i was 17
i came home on leave &
when i was getting ready to catch a flight back
my mother literally pinned the envelope with my
plane ticket to the inside of my suit coat

when my mother died
i thought i was going to go crazy
banged my head against the inside car window
at the funeral i was sitting in the front row
next to my sister & brothers & i thought
"i wish everyone would leave & let me be alone
with my mother"
years later at a family reunion i told that
to my sister dorothy & she said "why, harry,
why didn't you tell us, we would have gone
outside & let you be alone with mother"

when i turned 60
i began receiving a monthly s.a.g. pension

in the last week
i saw "blow," "the tailor of panama," "chopper,"

"keep the river on your right" & "memento"
growing up, i went to many movies with mother
last night, at the los feliz
i put my head in my hands, "i miss my mother"

4 26 01

my papers purchased

today, steve coy drove up
from la jolla & picked up
my professional & personal papers,
correspondence & manuscripts,
& took them to the mandeville
special collections library,
u.c.s.d., la jolla
27 boxes
162 springback binders, folders
& notebooks of my poetry & some prose
36 years' work
new york city, santa monica,
west hollywood, east hollywood
& various towns, cities, countries
where i worked as an actor

a sense of calm has come over me
after a 90 degree day, it was refreshingly
cool tonight
as i walked to western & sunset & back
past two hispanic church services
in sunset storefronts

from a venice storefront poetry center
to an octagonal library
with blackburn, oppen & rakosi

11 21 02

night color

in the black bedroom
i picked the pen i thought
was the blackest of the two
on my blue desk

in the living room
with the 3 150 watt bulbs on
i saw it was red

blood darker than black

12 4 02

to catch her sleep

our gray female cat
with white feet
curls up in my lap
she's relaxed in the middle
of the night
santa anas quiet
the trees & electrical poles down

short-haired
& with a farm odor

two years ago
she broke her back left leg
in the rain on the roof
& my wife nursed her
back to health
for six weeks
her leg in a cast

when the study door
where she was sequestered
opened a crack
& the outside window was open
she moved quickly toward freedom
dragging her leg like frankenstein

1 7 03

except for herky-jerky, hand-held

i was flipping channels today at 3:35 p.m.
& "crazy / beautiful" was on a movie
channel
rich, sexy, white girl falls in love with
handsome, mexican boy from east l.a.
i had seen this film advertised a couple
of years ago, but had never seen it

i missed the beginning, but watched
the rest of the movie — totally
captivated by it
kirsten dunst was the young girl

time went by without me knowing it
soon, it was 4:45 & then the movie was over

whenever a good movie comes on,
i feel like some older men feel
when they see a sexy, young girl
i get captivated, excited — a passion
comes over me

i have a passion for movies

last night, i saw "antwone fisher"
at the grove — a deeply, moving picture
i cried three times
at one emotional break through
i began writing a confession
in my mind: "i'm sorry i hated
. . ." & i did a litany of my bad deeds
confessing to denzel & those i have
liked but who have not cared for me
it was well written (the movie),
well acted & directed — the most
emotional film of the year

last week, i saw the violent,
heartless, youthful "city of god"
& "quai de lefevres," clouzot's

1947 mystery with louis jouvet —
masterful film-making

i watch a movie a day at home
on cable, or video from a studio,
or at the academy, or movie theatre

whenever i am not acting, writing,
reading, watching a movie, sports
event or news, i feel disconnected

"movies are your passion," she said

2 5 03

A Country Away

12-25-02 to 7-9-03

a country away

my brother, jim, paid for airline
tickets for holly & me
to visit him & his wife, mae, dec. 25th-
dec. 30th, at their home in raleigh
my brother, bob, & his wife, shio, who
live nearby
my sister, dorothy, & her husband, jim,
will get together with us
children & grandchildren will
be with us
we will drive to virginia to see
my oldest brother, georgie, & his wife,
margaret
we will see their children &
grandchildren

we are in the air near charlotte
we left our 4 cats at 5 a.m. in l.a.
my oldest brothers & sister were born
in the 1920s

holly & i have aisle seats across from
each other
she reads *the new yorker*
i read a bio of burroughs by b. miles

george, bob & dorothy grew up together
jim was born in 1938 & i was born
in 1940
jim has been helpful to me, financial-
ly, at needful times, over the years
fbi, presbyterian, ibm, farm,
movies

12 25 02

a beckoning

a poem is a group of words
that has an apple tied to its head
the asian diet bicycle
a friend who distinguishes
by putting his right foot inside
your right foot
a way to walk, with self reliant
niceties

a poem never vulgarizes spirit
by resting its math on monthly savings
or by counting its weekly payroll

the size of a bed remains stretched
with folding air by closing the
tightest ropes

bodies no longer old breathe love
with forgiving prayers
mountains clean
the old bodies do come around
two long walks a day

12 25 02

plane home

an hour into the flight
a u.s. air attendant pushed
a cart with white sacks on top
up the aisle
"what is that?" i asked
"dinner"
a small roll filled with
cheese & sliced turkey
a sugar cookie
mustard for the sandwich

later after dinner
a cart with drinks
came up the aisle
i got a cup of apple juice
& one of water

glad i ate a good healthy salad
of spinach, tomatoes, mushrooms
with italian dressing
& fresh corn, & tomato & onion
soup for lunch
at the "fresh tomato"

the reunion was great
jim & mae were warm, giving &
generous
a beautiful, clean, 2-story house

the night we arrived
we ate prime rib, scalloped potatoes,
string beans & drank champagne
i had a slice of mae's white cake
with decaf
doug, lisa, kevin, scott & stacey
were also at jim & mae's

thursday, i paid for a seafood
dinner at outback's

sat. morning jim drove us north
four hours to stay at a motel
in woodbridge, virginia
& eat at an italian restaurant
mae, dorothy & jim gay went with us

there were 20 at the dinner
to my left: dorothy, doug, lindsay,
shea, steve, jan, stacey, jimmie, george,
across from me & moving right:
margaret, jim gay, lisa, jill, donn,
at the end of the table: scott,
then mae, bryan, kevin,
holly — next to me

after a good meal
i ate veal picata
we told family memories
then 15 of us went to the motel
where jimmie asked if we could
use the room off the lobby
which is used for breakfast
"yes, until 11 p.m."

jim said, "why don't we start
with dorothy & go around to
the left & each one of us
say what you do each day &
what is the most important
thing that you did this past year"

i was third
"some of you know a 1ittle about
this — the university of california,
san diego, at la jolla, purchased
my professional & personal papers,
correspondence & manuscripts,
which are housed in the mandeville
special collections library.
what this means is they took
my books (published), cds, &
lit mags, newspapers, anthologies
that my poems are in, they
also have 207 pages of mother's
letters to me the last 4 years
of her life: 1966-1970. i

asked the director if she
wanted them & she said 'yes,
some people may think them
irrelevant, but if someone
were to write about you, he,
or she, could find out a lot about
your family & the little town
you came from, from her letters.'
i also told her: 'i have 36
movie scripts & 41 tv scripts, with
my notes, call sheets & photos, would
you be interested in them?' 'yes, we
want the whole you.' it is truly
an honor for my work to be in
a great library. i am also
deeply thankful to be part
of this family."

this was the first time i ever
talked to my family about my
poetry being published since
my first book, *amarillo born,*
was published in 1966 & i was
hurt by georgie's letter to me
& by bobbie not wanting to
take *amarillo born* home

an admission, a confession, a
speaking truth

12 30 02

born in the midwest

it becomes clear to me
that caring & compassion
are necessary for good hearted-
ness to engender love

when holly & i went to raleigh, n.c.
& woodbridge, va. to be with my
3 brothers & sister & their families
we experienced a loving family

everyone loves & cares for each
other & gives
in our rare time together
we sit in a circle & tell important

things to each other & listen

the gray cat emerges from the
butterscotch shawl draped
over my legs
she looks up at the old male cat

on my lap
where i lay my head
my mother's lap on car trips

1 4 03

cats & poets

the gray female cat
sits on a rust colored shawl
that covers my legs
she turns & curls her body
in my lap

tonight i watched "the
emperor's club" with kevin kline
he plays a history teacher
in a prep school
a film about virtue & lying
& cheating — character as fate
concealment, deception, riches,
devotion, confession

it was once said, "if a woman
were to tell the truth, the world
would split open"
many women have told the truth
& the world has not split open
i say, if poets in l.a. ever worked
together & cared for each other,
the world would split open

our 4 cats live together in peace
some times the 2 females fight
& the young gray cat hides
behind the oven
but mostly food & warmth &
kindness keep our brood happy

at times the 2 young cats
romp through the house
the night, sleep, cats —
no words to lie with
my hand on her back
her body on my wife's shawl
the shawl spread over my legs
in the night we stay together
for the warmth of words

words in our bodies connected
a wave to my wife through
the continuation behind sleep

3 1 03

According to her

To be fair
I called to remind him
It's more like
It's kinda like
No it was
Then again
Assuming he's coming back
He walked out the door
The way she described it
A lot of him
We were wondering
That's why I asked her
And also
Got to have it
No matter what
I'm sure she's watching
I don't think he would have
Inside outside
Got a rack for the night
Everything's referred to
A siren

3 12 03

manzanola

we moved to manzanola when i was
eleven
we had been living at 21-h in ord-
ville
i had been attending the sixth
grade at brownson, 2 miles away

daddy got a job in pueblo, colo.
daddy, mother, jimmie & i moved
into a house in manzanola
jim & i slept in a murphy bed
we used an outhouse
daddy drove forty miles to work

i remember there was a park
in the middle of town
a soda fountain where i used
to get butterscotch malts
made by the high school quarter-
back
manzanola had a population of
500
its high school football team
was coached by eddie troxel
& was a great football team
in division b
lot of strong farm boys
jimmie played on the team

i was in the last semester
of the sixth grade in manzanola
& i also attended seventh grade there

we moved into a better house in
manzanola
jimmie & i slept in the same bed
he would pinch me
tell daddy that i was pinching him
& daddy would come into our bed-
room & hit me

i had a paper route: *rocky mountain news* — 21 daily & 95 sunday
i saved my money & bought a
maroon english racer
delivered the daily papers on it
later i caught my foot in one
of the paper bags hanging over
the handlebars & wrecked the
bike, twisting the thin front tire
& wheel
the bike had cost fifty bucks
daddy drove me on sundays
we'd get up at four
he'd let me out with several
thick papers
drive ahead
pick me up

he taught me to drive in that 1949
2-door, maroon plymonth
when i was twelve

at one time, i delivered papers
after school on a horse
bareback

i played saxophone in the band
we went to pueblo for band day
i had gotten a mohawk
the band director made me
always wear my cap

i went out for the junior high
team at quarterback
on one early play, a defensive
player dug his shoulder in my stomach,
drove me backward, picked me up
& slammed me down
ending my thoughts of playing
football

i played softball
we had a real good pitcher
with a fancy delivery
billy eckhardt was his name

i had a friend named ronnie johnson
who dressed up in a cowboy outfit
with fringes on his shirt
played guitar & sang "jambalya"

i hitchhiked to rocky ford
eight miles away
sat in the back of a pickup
with watermelons
rocky ford was the watermelon
capital

we would drive to pueblo with daddy
at times
& see shacks with tv antennas
with fine cars in front
alongside the highway

pretty farm girls, football, ice cream
i played basketball in the gym

i would come home after school
& watch tv in our second home
though i remember watching
a heavyweight fight in 1951 or '52
through a gas station window

i moved with my family from town
to town

3 23 03

trip to lincoln

when i was a junior
ron gilbreath, 2 other classmates
& i went to lincoln, 358 miles
east of sidney, to see the high
school basketball playoffs
we all had played basketball together
on the high school team

we left thur. after school
i had cashed 2 u.s. savings bonds —
that i had won in 2 "i speak for
democracy" contests — worth $35

we stopped in kearney about 9 p.m.
& visited larry edwards
who was going to nebr. state college
his room had a bed, sofa, table & chair,
& a slanted roof
larry was 2 years ahead of us at s.h.s.
he had played fullback on the h.s. team

we drove on to lincoln, arriving late
at night, & checked into a motel
the next day ronnie went to see his
girl, who was a student at n.u.

the next 3 days & 2 nights
we drank & partied, visited fraternity
& sorority houses
saw a couple of high school games
i even saw wilt chamberlain
he played for kansas u. against nebr. u.
i sat right behind the basket

i ate big hamburgers at drive-ins
i stole 2 quarts of beer from
a bar, ran & slid under a car
to hide & ruined a beautiful
tan suede jacket

coming home late sunday night
i syphoned gas from cars along
the way & even in ordville
before i went home

mother smelled the gas in my mouth
as i lay in bed
all night i had that gas taste
in my mouth before i finally fell asleep

5 4 03

today

i went to jay's flowers
at farmers market & bought
my wife a bunch of lilacs
to celebrate our 13th wedding
anniversary this monday

i bought 2 chocolate mousse
for us

at 5:30, we drove to moca
& saw lucien freud's paintings
big portraits, powerful, acutely real
though the nudes aren't as beautiful
as matisse's female
freud's focused
memorable work

our home: woman sleeping in bed
3 cats sleep on newly restored couch
1 female by my side
heat on, quiet, almost midnight
a thousand reasons to hold her hand
as we walk on grand

5 8 03

locate the cats

junior sleeps on top of the filing
cabinet
joey lies on the southern end
of the brown sofa, rose on the
northern
joey gets up, leaps down to
the wooden floor, walks into the
study
egypt cleans herself on the western
pillow of the love seat
joey enters the living room
he licks his mouth
he washes his outer right leg
joey walks to the black chest
leaps up on it
he turns his head, washes his
upper right leg
harry sits on top of a white cover
& a green cover
on the middle pillow of the brown
sofa
an accidental autobiography
the selected letters of
gregory corso
next to his right leg

6 1 03

night in june

the boy in the hooded sweatshirt
tells his grandpa the type of car
in the next freeway lane

his mother enjoys her first visit
to l.a.
his sister points out a half moon
to their mother
as they emerge from chavez ravine

a swift pitch, fans standing
chilly june night

a victory for the home team
part of a family united
santa monica to long beach to
venice
to beverly hills, east hollywood
silver lake, echo park

uncle bought tickets, brought
pillows, aunt brought cookies
four guessed attendance
politeness, giving, family love

6 6 03

the archaeologist of sleeping cats

the boy doesn't want to be on the
pier. he wants to go back to the hotel.
he's cold. he wears shorts & a hooded
sweatshirt. gray as l.a.'s june gloom.

his granduncle had hugged a nephew,
niece-in-law, grandniece & grandniece
the day before. the family giggled.
it was an innocent love.

the blonde mother walked in the cold
pacific on a night in early june.
the water was colder than the atlantic.

used musical instruments were taken
to haiti & given to poor people who
were musicians.

a man read robert lowell's poetry in
east hollywood. he was surrounded by
3 sleeping cats. the young gray female
cat walked around the room. she put
her face near the old gray & white
male cat's face.

the two brothers sat across from each
other in the broadway deli in santa
monica. the older brother ate meat
loaf. the younger brother ate white
fish, mashed potatoes & vegetables.
his wife ate a rock shrimp pizza.
the older brother was the richer
one he paid.

he also paid to have the faces drawn
of his daughter-in-law, grandson &
granddaughter. the grandson was
happy while the artist on the pier
drew his likeness. other times, on
the pier, the teenager was cold. he
wanted to go back to the hotel.

two young hispanic men, one had a
brown pit bull on a leash, walked by,
"look out for the mean pit bull."

there were not many people on
the pier. the old male cat walks
the length of the sofa & settles
next to the mother cat. he jumps
down & goes into the study where
the food, water & 2 litter boxes are.

6 6 03

l.a. visit: brother, his daughter-in-law, & 2 of her children

white fish, mashed potatoes, vegetables
a walk to the pier

curried chicken sandwich, salad
aquarium — 2 otters play like kitties
1 rolls in the water, wipes his mouth &
whiskers with his paws

hot dog & bud light
dodgers beat the white sox 2-1, friday night
lisa's first major league game
my brother, jim, sits next to me, holly
next to him — later, holly sits behind me

john dorry on mashed potatoes at the
lobster, holly had ahi tuna, jim had
salmon, lisa — scallops, her children
ate filet mignon with french fries
later, they had their palms read &
cards read by natalie at doreena's

poached eggs, potatoes, 1 sausage, o.j.
& coffee for sunday breakfast
at the doubletree
venice boardwalk, san vicente to
bundy, left to sunset, right
over the 405, past ucla to beverly
hills, past the beverly hills hotel,
right on alpine, right on santa monica
blvd, left on rodeo — "there's the
beverly wilshire hotel" — right on
wilshire

whitley to sunset, right
later, pointed out laurel ave. where
fitzgerald lived
the directors' guild
left on la brea to hawthorne, right
parked, walked to grauman's chinese
looked at the footprints: monroe's,
norma shearer's, cooper's … the

stars among the tourists
visited the kodak
walked up the stairs, pointed out 1991
"the silence of the lambs"
a smoothie — then back to the white
town car — hollywood to vine, right
to sunset, right to amoeba
bought scott & stacey each a cd
back to santa monica via santa monica blvd

jim, lisa, scott, stacey
came to our home at 5
holly cooked macaroni & cheese for
stacey
holly put out 2 salads she had made
i broiled cheeseburgers
we had lemon meringue pie from
du par's
holly & lisa sat on the patio & talked
jim, stacey & i watched the last
quarter of the nba playoffs, the spurs
won
scott laid down on the sofa with his
purple slippers on & listened to his new
rap cd

"did you give harry a hug, scott & stacey?
we hug each other in our family"

6 10 03

she returned on father's day

father's day yesterday
& it seemed like a year long day
when i got up at 6 a.m.
i fed the cats, opened the drapes
saw rose — who had been gone
for 11 days & let her in
woke holly to tell her
the good news
holly was thrilled
& defrosted some turkey
in the microwave oven for her

i wrote poetry
walked to sears
bought 2 pairs of shorts —
1 black 1 white
& 2 pairs of navy socks
slept, found a box on a kitchen shelf
that had my notes & writing
from milton, english 420, my last
college course at c.s.u.n. in 1984

watched the final pro basketball
game of the season — spurs won
& ate a superb 1/2 chicken with herbs,
garlic & mushrooms
from farfalla
it came with roasted potatoes & green
beans & carrots
holly had the same

pretty orange roses in a vase
on the round brown wooden table

rose sits on my lap
brown ears, black top of head
black top of body
white left side of body
black tail with white & brown
brown face with white lower

half
white & brown feet

6 16 03

4 decades

i get up at 4:45 a.m.
read *an accidental autobiography,*
the selected letters of gregory corso
heat on, 3 cats up, 1 sleeps
2 of them run around the house
2 want out — it's too early

last night, i saw "man on the train,"
a french film with jean rochefort
& johnny hallyday — an intriguing
film: train, town, poetry, robbery,
2 opposites, guns, companionship

13 days ago, i met jonathan demme
at paramount
he had fedexed a copy of "the
manchurian candidate" to me
two days before

i showed him 2 photos of me
when i played the governor of kansas
in the movie, "kansas," 16 years ago
he passed the photos to the screenwriter
& casting director, & then gave them
back to me
there was an american flag in each photo
when i left the meeting room
& was standing in an outer room
the casting director came out
& asked me for the photos
"i wanted jonathan to have these
because i would like to play gov.
arthur, so i am glad you asked
for them. jonathan always has
great taste, so whatever he has in
mind for me will be fine."

jonathan has hired me 9 times
as an actor

during the meeting, jonathan said,
"we will find a part for you in the movie"

after a movie at the los feliz

"the only thing better than
bowling is pool," a young woman
said
on vermont
6 young italian men drink espresso
at an outside table at palermo's
the bar in "vermont" is full of
young men & women
a gray bearded man begs for
money outside skylight books
a college-age woman wearing
low cut red converse asks for
change at a corner on vermont
a man eats sea bass, polenta &
asparagus at figaro's outside
his wife eats mussels & french
fries
a 62-year-old man wearing an
hawaiian shirt looks through the
glass of skylight books at an
orange cat
9 p.m. on a tuesday night in east
hollywood

6 26 03

a clarity

at 3:01 a.m., i was sitting on
the brown sofa in our living room
joey, our old gray cat was purring
in my lap
i rubbed his back
as i read corso's letters

two honks
i went into the bedroom, looked
out the window & saw a van
stopped in the street

i put my wranglers on
& walked out the door & up to
the van
2 armenian men in it

"excuse me, could you please
walk up to the door & knock,
instead of honking every night,
because you wake my wife up,
& me, & the neighbors?"

"yes, ok, i'm sorry, sir"

6 26 03

a journey

past an armenian mother
& her two teenage daughters
past mrs. arrieta, who has grown
"emotionally old" because her
lovely 30-year-old daughter, grace,
has ms
past more armenians
one a watch/clock repair man
past a filipino tailor
a thai restaurant
a one stop market owned by a young
hispanic man
to edgemont — with a baptist church
northwest corner
past a gypsy family with a large, shiny
red pickup parked on their front
concrete
past a greek shoe repair man
an outdoor armenian cafe
the headquarters of scientology
scientologists tending to flower beds
& lawns like eager mormons
past a filipino cafe
the best omelets in town
to fountain & vermont

6 30 03

memorial to al at jans

i met al maines in 1968, or 1969, at
the old world restaurant on the strip

he lived with his friend & fellow actor,
tony king, on san vicente, just south
of sunset boulevard
al & tony studied acting with stella
adler in new york city

al was a tap dancer from newburgh, n.y.
he loved fred astaire
he knew & loved old musicals
knew all the numbers
knew what clothes fred astaire wore
in each movie
he modeled his dress on fred astaire

i was at the old world the night
he met martine, who would become
his wife, & have their child, yolanda
martine was young & pretty with
long, dark-brown hair

in the early '70s, they lived on laurel,
on the east side of the street,
between fountain & sunset
martine worked, al took care
of yolanda
al would put on his yellow cardigan
over a brooks brothers' shirt
he would wear gray flannels
& spectator shoes, & walk to schwab's
holding yolanda's hand
he was like a mother to her

i remember one time my wife & i
& our young son, dylan, visited al,
martine & yolanda
the children must have been 2 or 3
they played in yolanda's room
while we adults were in the living

room
after a while, we checked on them
& they were both naked & covered
with baby powder & there was
baby powder all over the room
they were bouncing up & down
on the bed when we came into the
room

al & i were friends for many years
he helped me with many auditions
& many acting jobs
he came up with great ideas
for clothes, actions, tenor of the scene

for "new york, new york," he suggested
that my character wear a hearing aid
because the character had lost his
hearing in the second world war
we went to a hearing aid specialist
& i bought a 1945 hearing aid
scorsese loved it for my character

years later, when i went to phila-
delphia to read for the sheriff in
"beloved," he suggested that i wear
new, pressed, light-blue wranglers,
dress boots, white western shirt, navy
cashmere blazer
that i have long hair, long side-
burns
i did what he suggested & demme asked
me to be the sheriff after the read-
ing — al also ran lines with me

al loved coffee shops
he used to hang out at one on 54th
& seventh in manhattan
he loved food, especially steak, a
thick porterhouse
he loved spaghetti
he worked at paddy's clam house
in n.y.c.
he worked as a waiter at the old
world
he was a counterman at turner's

on the strip
he used to hang out at argo's
on santa monica blvd & orange drive
he lived on curson above willoughby
for many years

we used to go to movies together
we would hang out at his place
go to coffee shops: kings road cafe,
broadway deli, rose cafe, schwab's,
theodore, argo's, farmers market,
canter's

in 1987, al suggested that i
talk to the owners of gasoline alley
on melrose about starting a poetry
reading series
which i did & they said yes
& i coordinated the "poetry on melrose"
every sunday for 18 months
2 poets read ½ hour each
occasionally 1 read 45 minutes
& then i passed the hat
a successful venture
& al came to many of the readings
his favorite was robert peters
doing his "blood countess"
peters memorized the 45-minute work
& wore a dress

al liked the 7-layer cake at canter's

floyd mutrux hired al for several
movies
al appeared in "hill street blues"
he acted in a movie of the week
with sid caesar & milton berle

al taught tap to tony bennett
he taught tap to janice rule
he had a tap dance studio on fairfax
he had a tap dance studio on yucca

in the mid-seventies, al came home
one day & saw his wife holding their
daughter, yolanda, & his wife's lawyer

carrying al's color tv
they were getting into the lawyer's
mercedes
that was the last time al saw
yolanda for many years
martine & yolanda moved to corpus
christi
al took a bus to corpus christi
to visit yolanda several years later
in a functional, court-appointed
visit in a court waiting room
yolanda visited al briefly when she
was 17 — her main purpose was to
visit a marine in san diego —
when she left, she said, "so long, al"

al died at age 66 at cedars-sinai
he was born in newburgh, n.y.
his sisters, marilyn & vaughn,
sat at a long table at jans
with 30 friends of al's on july 1, 2003
who shared memories of al

i had not been close with al
the last 4 or 5 years because of a
falling out, but i always had
warm feelings for him during that
time

7 1 03

ritual

the planes flew over in formation
while a fireman sang the national
anthem
& in a later inning
the pilots & crew stood in front
of the home team's dugout

bing cherries
baked potato chips
bottled water
dodger dog with mustard & relish
bud light in plastic bottle
brownie from greenblatt's

the dodgers lost to the snakes
fell farther back
2 young mexican gang guys sat
their heads in their hands

earlier, when gagne trotted on
the field, the place erupted
fans stood
he held the diamondbacks
for half an inning

55,038
fireworks afterward
right in our face
top deck

a slow exit
john & i talked about schwartz,
jarrell, lowell, berryman, roethke,
fiedler, discernment

"you are good friends," i said
as john drove his wife, dorothy,
holly & me home on sunset
in their big, wide, red, american car

7 5 03

living room floor

sleep dream sidney home town
nebraska panhandle
stole tape recorders stole
gasoline stole rifle stole
bullets

backed '51 black chevy
into farm
pumped gas into car
dirt road off highway 30

disrupted nature
destroyed winter wheat
drove car on fields
shot jack rabbits

threw baseballs threw rocks threw
tomatoes threw snowballs

played war with m1 rifle stock
took .22 rifle into hills & shot
at wooden posts tin cans prairie
dogs rabbits windmills

planned robberies ran away

dream baseball dream lawyer
played baseball softball basket-
ball swam ran fell rode horses

wrote speeches memorized speeches
won contests
acted in community & high school plays

worked in fields thinning beets
worked in chinese laundry
was clothing salesman
pumped gas drove a tractor

fell in love
her face was hot against mine

hitchhiked 12 miles from s.o.d. to sidney
dozens of times
went to movies played pool went
swimming danced drank beer
played pool

broke our front door window with
my fist
opened door from inside, fell drunk

7 7 03

memory present

when i was growing up
i fell in love with barbara
robinson, sandy lewis, diane
devier, carolyn mcgirr

danced with sandy, diane, carolyn
they were all pretty
now, i'm 62, live in east hollywood
my wife, holly, also from nebraska
has given me many years of happiness,
love & care
we have been together 25 years
& made love thousands of times
she's a gracious & exciting lover
i praise her love & i praise her body
i praise her soul

at times i have failed
humility has been my companion
in my youth i ran away
my body flushed

i sit in our home, 3:32 a.m.
2 cats beside me, my wife asleep
a body hits the front door
the cats & i look up
a young man drunk?
someone trying to break in?
i turn out the light & look out
see nothing but a light on
in an upstairs apartment

the body of woman has been grace
a wheat field to hide in
hills to play in
to get away from houses & cars
to be alone in the dark with
a lonely existence to be within

a sheet a down quilt the fan off
trees tornadoes tears
my wife has the largest heart of mine

7 7 03

solace

i cherish windmills of youth
pound said never use an abstract at
the end of a preposition
i cherish the apricots on the table
with lemons limes oranges in a bowl
i hear voices from an adjoining
apartment at 3:36 a.m.
tears fall from my eyes as i remember
love & sports & trouble from my boyhood

i am no longer young
my life is composed of reading &
writing, watching movies, loving my
wife & cats

poetry readings, auditions, reading
from the *bible,* walks along fountain
& sunset, baseball games, lunches
with actors & comedians

i am no longer young
but i am solid
my body is clean & my soul repairs
all the abstract burnings, failings,
yearnings — repairs by folding & re-
arranging & hearing the flights
of a legal conscience
assigned to shining a light on
the running away
from breaking, deceit &
a longing to be honest & finite

a sexual human thing
a heart in light, solace alone in the
3 directions

7 7 03

pal joey

my cat, joey, gives me solace
he sits on my lap & i pet him,
scratch his upper back, he purrs
it's 2:20 a.m., wed.

when we first got joey, andrea
called his color "mousey gray"
he has a beautiful white ruff
white nose pink tip white mouth
white feet white belly & neck

we first saw joey leaping in & out
of the apartment window just south
of our driveway — he lived with 2 guys
they moved & abandoned him
holly captured him brought him home

he's the patriarch, must be about 16,
& gets along well with the other 3 cats
at times he sits next to junior &
joey licks junior's head & neck & then
bites him & wrestles with him
junior's good-natured, bigger than joey,
puts up with it for awhile, waves his
bushy tail, then gets up & walks away

7 9 03

The Night Has Always Been A Friend

7-20-03 to 11-26-03

a rare reflection

each night i rise at midnight
or later & read corso's lovely,
emotionally honest, erudite in
terms of poesy, soul-to-soul letters.
or i read them at farmers market
among the plums, cheese danishes,
fresh poultry & pies. or i read them
at an outside table at the silver spoon.

corso's letters may be better than
his poems, though without his poems no
letters, without his life no poems. his
20 to 30 youth (1950-1960), a muse-union
with allen ginsberg, a magnificent
outpouring of poetry followed by letters.

listening is essential to acting.
it is also essential to poetry, love &
camaraderie. and it is rare in poetry.

7 20 03

her first film: "you came along"

sunday, july 20th, 2003,
i, along with holly, picked up
lizabeth scott
at her home above the chateau marmont

she was dressed immaculately in gray
& beige
she had long blonde hair
she looked lovely

her home had recently suffered
water damage
& many of her books had been soaked,
including 2 signed, first editions
of frost's poetry

frost won 4 pulitzers, i said

we talked, as i drove south on crescent
heights, over to la cienega, left to
venice, right

she began as a model
had 5 photos in *harper's bazaar*
did broadway

i loved you in "dead reckoning"
& "the strange love of martha
ivers," i said. i believe john
cromwell directed "dead reckon-
ing" & lewis milestone directed
". . . martha ivers"

boy, you know your movies, she
said

harry's an actor, he loves movies,
holly said

we talked going & coming back
& while we were at beyond baroque,

i introduced her to fellow poets
& most knew her & praised her

after the reading, she & i hugged
she was happy & said, you were won-
derful, what vitality, your voice
was so vibrant, you were the best

we ate cake
it was a joyous time

7 21 03

Premonition: 10 Years & Suicide

Kobe Bryant being charged
with 1 count of sexual assault,
a felony, is the saddest thing
in L.A. sports' history.
No one could leap as high, hang
in the air as long, go up against
a big man, do acrobatic moves,
hit the 3, come up with the big
play on defense as he could.
He was an Egyptian king.
He was as much a prince as Miles
Davis.
He had a flair about him.
He moved diagonally down the court.
Lean & tall & young & confident &
mature & focused.
Until June 30th, 2003, in Colorado.

Magic, being HIV-positive, stopped
at age 31. That was a shock. But
that was/is an illness.
Bob Marley, whom a friend thought
Kobe resembled, died at 36.

But Kobe's case, to me, resembles
James Dean. Dean made 3 films &
died in a car crash at age 24.
Kobe is 24 & has won 3 NBA
championships with the Lakers.

I was a teenager when I saw Dean
in "Rebel Without A Cause."
I thought that he was such a
mature actor at such a young age.
I thought wouldn't you have liked
to have had a brother like him?
He had so much understanding.

I am 62 now & when Kobe was
on TV with his wife & 2 lawyers

& he said, "… I am innocent …"
I felt like he was my son. He
admitted that he had committed
adultery, he apologized to his wife,
but he denied using any force
with his accuser. He said the sex
was "consensual."

My heart broke. He was so young &
talented. A streak across the
heaven.

7 22 03

pismo beach motel

the parking lot next to
the beachcomber inn, where we
are staying, is almost full
on a friday afternoon

we drove up from l.a. to pismo beach
yesterday — left at 10 a.m., stopped
at summerland for lunch,
arrived at 1:50 p.m.

we made love in the afternoon
walked on the pier
ate at rosa's
watched tv & fell out at 10:10 p.m.

out the motel window
i see a truck with "pacific seafood"
printed on its side
a boy, with a surfboard balanced
on his head, walking toward the ocean
beginning of the pier
the blue pacific

this afternoon i walked in the ocean
my wife & i love the west coast
she sleeps, her head & left hand &
forearm visible

8 1 03

he loved to play cribbage

my father wanted peace & quiet
when he came home
he worked as a property supply
manager at sioux ordnance depot
after he retired from the civil
service, he worked as a bartender

daddy, i called him
he invited eddie raulinitis to dinner
& eddie ate 4 polish sausages
my friend, conrad ribera, was one
of simon's 11 children
& daddy would often ask conrad
to stay for dinner
after conrad & i had been playing
marbles or catch
even though daddy had disparaging
things to say about mexicans

daddy worked hard his whole life
drank beer, read westerns, did
crossword puzzles, read crime maga-
zines
he was short, had a big belly, skinny
legs
when i was stationed in hawaii
in the navy, i sent him a pair of
brown, chief petty officer's shoes
& a $144 short wave, around the world,
radio
he kept the radio by his bed

he kept his false teeth in a glass of
water
he was clean shaven
he used mennen after shave lotion

daddy liked to drive
he owned a 1949 maroon, 2-door
plymouth, a 1952 light-blue, 4-door

belvedere, a 1955 studebaker
station wagon

he kept the kitchen cabinets full of food
he & mother were excellent cooks
he had 1 rule: no arguments at the
dinner table

8 20 03

george

my father asked me to walk on his back
he would put his chin in his left hand,
his right hand atop the back of his head
& sharply, quickly, turn his head to the left
he dreamed of going to mineral baths
in another state
he wore brown corduroys
he would get us up early & get out on the
road

daddy tended bar at the mill, the silver
dollar, brandin' iron, elk's club, brown-
son tavern
he drank beer, at 7:30 a.m., at boyd's cigar
store
he drank beer, on saturdays, at the log
cabin

daddy used to say to me, "you would lie
when the truth would serve better"

he & mother played cribbage with the nick
noles & ben boles — both couples
looked like daddy & mother

he hand-fed raw hamburger to nipsie & dollie

8 20 03

elaine

we used to visit elaine in la jolla.
she lived on fay right across
from la jolla high school.
at one time she had a deep lawn
before the city widened the street
in front of her place & took part
of her lawn.
she lived in a zero drug tolerance
zone.
the area she lived in had been
planned to be turned into a freeway
but never was.
her rent was moderate.
she would let us sleep in the bed-
room & she would sleep on a bed
in the living room.
she had a charming cat named
scoop, who would stand on her
back feet & paw at the wind with
her front paws. a lovely dance.
large living room, an area where
she kept her books & research
material, table & chair.
kitchen, which was never immac-
ulate.
bedroom, long hall & bathroom.
big picture window. a comfortable
& cool place.
we would stay for four days or a
week.
we would take her out to eat.
drive to scenic places, to balboa park,
san diego, ucsd, la jolla.
we met several of her friends from
aa.
for many years, elaine worked as
a marine biologist at scripps.
at least 20, before the grant ended.
then she taught, part time, at nearby

colleges.
she studied nature in vacant lots,
hill tops — fought encroaching real
estate ventures into city's nature.
got written up for her iconic, nature-
loving stance. researched & recorded
flora & fauna. she guided us over
her temporal victories.
she had 1 large, new bottle of coco
chanel perfume & 1 old.
she had many pairs of colored
dungarees & numerous plaid shirts
hanging in the bedroom closet.
my wife had attended albion college
in michigan with her.
elaine was slender, tall, had a
tender face, an ingratiating smile.
a distinctive laugh.
somewhat carefree as a homemaker,
a friendly person.
she was diagnosed with brain cancer
a year & a half ago & was given
6 months to live. she died a month
ago.
we had last seen her a year ago
when we stayed with her.
she had 2 things she wanted to do
with us. we watched a video of "trip
to bountiful" (holly & elaine
laid on the bed, i sat in a chair
next to the bed as we watched the
video). & then she sat on the living
room floor as she played an audio
cassette recording of her brother giving
a eulogy at their father's funeral.
specifics & birds & fish & laughter.
i walked to wind 'n sea many times
each time we visited elaine.

8 21 03

the darkness before the light

1
the light in the night
is inside with the cats

it is equally alone with hemingway's
letters & biographies on martin luther
king, jr., charles dickens & joyce

a woman calls up & the man says
"what about me? i'm a human being, too"
he tells her that he comes from a caring
family
he tries to tell her that friendship
contains give & take
she thinks that men do not care about
weddings
because today is the wedding of her
51-year-old son & her husband has
gone somewhere
& she tells him that her eldest brother
has given her 2 middle-age sons
$5,000 each

he shaves & washes his hair
& puts on a clean pair of wranglers
& a blue, silk hawaiian shirt from
ocean echo

he takes his reading glasses
& hemingway's letters with him
& he goes to the silver spoon
sits outside, & orders oatmeal
with low fat milk & sliced banana

while he's eating, an actor who
has done many broadway musicals
& 1 film, sits down & begins
criticizing scorsese's films

2
"scorsese hired me for his first
six films & his first tv show
it is an honor to have worked
with him"

he continues his attack & i point
out that "taxi driver" won the
palme d'or at cannes in 1976
& received a best picture nomination
by the academy in 1976

two other actors sit down &
they express their likes & dislikes

when i get home, i think what
a day & help my wife bring
the groceries in, walk around the house,
try to rest a little, tell her of my day
feel a little empty

about 4:30 p.m., on this friday,
my agent, kathleen schultz, calls
"i have an offer for you for 'the
manchurian candidate':
demme wants you for the part
of congressman flores, the name
will probably be changed,
a limousine will pick you up
you'll fly to new york on the 24th
you work on nov. 25th & 26th
it's thanksgiving week
the contract is $4,000 for a week
$100 a day per diem
you'll stay at the parker meridien
you fly first class
the reason it took so long for them
to get back to us is that 12 million
dollars were cut from the budget
only you & another actor are being
flown to new york from l.a."
"yes, thank you, kathleen"

holly & i talked about the deal
& the time — thanksgiving week
we were both very happy

demme hired me 3 times in the
seventies
3 times in the eighties
3 times in the nineties
1 time in the 21st century

demme had said, "we will find a role
for you in the film"
& he kept his word
he has always fulfilled his word

8 23 03

the night

the night has always been my friend
in west hollywood
i would write deep into the night
in santa monica
i would sit at the counter in zucky's
& read artaud in translation
in manhattan
i would go to movies on 42nd st at
2 a.m.
in sidney
i would sit in the east side cafe at
midnight, eating french fries & drinking
coke

these nights, i rise at midnight, 1, 2, 3 a.m.
& read hemingway's letters, corso's letters,
penguin lives
pet my cats, write my life

my life is love & baseball
reading amos from the *bible* out loud
walking on fountain to vermont
up to sunset, left to western
stop at a flower shop on the way home
& buy my wife an orange rose

i worked in "taxi driver" nights
in manhattan
at 45th & tenth, at the belmore
cafeteria, at the st. regis
i worked nights, 9, acting in "over
the edge," the climax, in greeley, colo.

wooden floor, fan on
the old male cat sleeps by the door
rose sleeps next to me on the sofa
junior sleeps on the other end

when i lived off-base for 2 months
in waikiki, i would wake in the middle

of the night, get a book & go sit in
the kitchen & read

on greyhound buses to & from new york
to sidney, i read *theatre arts* until i
was exhausted, slept, woke & read
plays, theatre history

the night has always been a friend
& i am with cats, my wife sleeps,
& i write, no longer alone

8 24 03

six sharing

in the night our hands are often
holding letters of famous writers
or movie reviews
our hearts are more often still & full
the young male cat by my side

day time has a cleanliness above all
six sets of hands on or below a table
a shadow mistaken for a tail

it was her first day of school
her husband cleaned their clothes
he bought hamburger, freshly baked
buns, 4 sharp cheddar cheese slices, corn
at the market
he cooked when she got home
"you make the best cheeseburgers"

the night has always been a friend
quiet, welcoming, open, cool

love, movies, drugs, walks, drives
the drugs were years ago, the love
continues
the young cat licks his thick fur
his eyes follow a fly
"you were brought here to love"
in four days i will be 63
"little junior & rose, i love my
kitties" — she jumps down, stretches
goes into the study
he gets up, walks to the spot where
she had been, smells, curls up

my life has a comfort seldom known
a home, a loving wife, work as an
actor, good health, pension, residuals,
money in the bank for medical
or dental emergencies, friends who
are poets, actors, directors,… a caring
brother, 4 cats, books, movies

i read out loud from the *bible* every
day, i walk 30 or 40 minutes several
times a week
my heart is clean
my hands are working hands

8 29 03

birthday

1
my 63rd birthday
is tuesday, sept. 2, 2003

tomorrow, sunday,
john & dorothy are coming
here at 5 p.m.
then holly & i will go
with them to la serenata de gari-
baldi — an early birthday
dinner celebration

tuesday, i will eat lunch
at the silver spoon with mike ford
afterward, i'll buy 3 brownies
at greenblatt's

tuesday night, i am going to
see the dodgers play the astros
with mark rhodes

holly has bought me a white shirt
from brooks brothers
holly, jim & mae, john & dorothy, &
phoebe have sent me birthday cards
phoebe's said "don't open till
sept. 2"

2
about 10:20 p.m., monday night,
i heard a barrage of gun shots
a few minutes later, i saw a
2-door, gray, 2000 honda with 3 guys
speed south on mariposa
10 minutes later, a police helicopter
appeared above to the south & began
to fly in a circle, shining its search-
light

two hours later, i walked to the
corner & saw that fountain was

blocked by police cars & taped off
at mariposa & normandie & i also
saw cops standing in vaco's driveway
& a cop in front of the fountain theatre

my neighborhood, my 63rd birthday

3
on labor day
the day before my 63rd birthday
my son, dylan, & his wife, michele,
called & wished me a happy birthday
they are having family over for
barbeque
tomorrow, dylan is taking a day off
from work to take the girls to school

georgie, my oldest brother, & his wife,
margaret, called to wish me happy
birthday
margaret said, "you were the one
we enjoyed seeing the most at the
family reunion dinner after christmas"
we talked about their 2 sons & their
families
"steve has a great sense of humor"

i called jimmie —
he had called me yesterday & wished
me a happy birthday —
we talked about the possibility
of me flying down to raleigh
after i finish working on "the
manchurian candidate" in new york
city on thanksgiving day & staying
with him & mae for 4 or 5 days
before returning to l.a.

on labor day
i wrote, took a 30 minute walk,
watched democrats & republicans,
who are running for governor &
president, give speeches on tv

i watched the dodgers lose 10-1 to
the astros

on labor day, 2003
i thought of my mother
who was in amarillo
getting ready to give birth to me

4
two nights ago, there were gun shots
half a block away
last night, mark rhodes & i went to
dodger stadium, saw l.a. beat houston
3–1 & move to 1½ games out of first place
in the wild card race
saw gagne come in with 2 out in the
8th & get the side out
& shut the astros down in the 9th
& set a major league record
with his 55th consecutive save

8 30 03
to
9 3 03

licks her paw & cleans her face

today, i had a nice day
shaved, showered,
washed my hair
went to western costumes
in north hollywood
for a fitting for "the
manchurian candidate"
mj measured me
& i told her i'd like to
wear a navy blue suit

then i went to the silver spoon
thanked robert forster
for recommending me
for "karen sisco"
"i auditioned for it thursday"
he said, "you don't need
to thank me, you're a good actor
in your own right"

i sat at an outdoor table,
ordered a bowl of lentil soup
ate it
mike mccarty sat down &
ordered a salad
we had a nice talk
his first broadway job
was in a tom stoppard play

later, dick miller & john regis
joined us
dick talked about movies
he had seen on sat. & sun.
at the academy

i sat at the silver spoon
from 11 a.m. to 1 p.m.
came home, napped for half
an hour, walked to citibank

holly cooked swordfish, spinach
& mashed potatoes — delicious supper
we watched the dodgers
beat the snakes 10-3
& are now 2 games out of first
in the wild card race

the weather has cooled
off a little

9 8 03

acting job

i'm happy to be working
playing sonny grodin, an ex-con,
on "karen sisco," a new tv series
being shot at universal

got to universal at 10:30 a.m.
call at 11, met john coles,
director, & rachel, 2nd a.d.,
she showed me my room

went to rehearsal, said hi
to robert forster, who plays
marshall, & frank pesce, poker
player — rehearsed, wardrobe

wardrobe liked my costume:
black pants, a green-1eaves-with-
cream-flowers-on-black-
background rayon hawaiian
shirt

went to make-up & hair
back to my room
shoot in 45 minutes

9 12 03

the intimate events of my life

i read the *l.a. times* in bed
every morning as i drink coffee
& pet pal joey

i love my wife's body
she goes to sleep at 10:30 p.m.
i go to bed with her
& usually wake up in an hour or so

our house is clean
& our hearts also

she is 65 & she teaches writing
in our home & teaches poetry at
usc
i am 63 & have made a modest living
as an actor for 28 years

a week & a half ago, at 10:15 p.m.
i heard 8 gun shots & saw a
speeding car go south on mariposa
two nights later, i walked by
6 candles on fountain between
normandie & mariposa where
an armenian gang guy had been
killed by an hispanic gang

the killing was half a block
from our home

intimate car sounds, intimate neigh-
bors' dogs barking, intimate nightly
police helicopters, intimate foreign
languages, intimate motorcycles

i love the intimacy of love amidst
all the city's intimacies

9 14 03

our last game of the season

when we got home from dodger
stadium, i watched the 8th & 9th
innings on tv
the giants won 6-4
each team had 11 hits
but the dodgers had made 2
errors on the first 2 plays

at 10:40, a helicopter hovered
high above us & stayed in one place
the noise was driving me crazy
the helicopter stayed there
for half an hour

when the 11 o'clock news came on
a tv anchor said there had
been an argument between a
giant fan & a dodger fan in
parking lot 27 at dodger stadium
& the dodger fan pulled out a gun
& shot & killed the giant fan
the cops were looking for a white suv

9 20 03

watering hole

"there are two things
you can't become in this town:
tired & bitter, because then
nobody will want to be with you,"
jimmie scrudato said about hollywood.

a bunch of us congregate at the silver
spoon daily at lunch time.
actors, television writer, comedians,
screenwriter, director.
inside table, outdoor table.

there used to be a group of us
who hung out at farmers market;
but that group has disassembled.

i go to the silver spoon once or twice
a week & sit at an outdoor table
with dick miller.
robert forster sits at a table next
to the western wall.

dodger stadium is a great place
to look at people as is farmers market.

silver spoon is down the street from
where i used to live.
i lived on havenhurst for 11 years.
silver spoon used to be called theodore.

i eat oatmeal with sliced banana &
low fat milk, or a turkey burger with
cole slaw, or a bowl of navy bean soup,
or a bowl of split pea soup.

martin landau ("north by northwest" &
"ed wood") was sitting outside &
3 of us couldn't remember his name.
"he knew james dean."
finally, his name came to one of us.

shelley winters celebrated her 83rd or
84th birthday on the patio, a while back.
she's missing half her teeth, is hunched
over a little, frail, but still vibrant.

kip doesn't come around anymore.
asher sits at the counter, reads the
sports section while he eats.

9 21 03

she stands & looks

the young gray cat
has all four feet
on one arm of the loveseat

she stands on her back feet
& looks for something in the
tiny alcove where 3 photos
of our grandchildren are
3 girls ages 8-11

she jumps up & sits sideways
in front of the photos
she turns her head upward
she looks downward

she jumps back down
to the arm of the loveseat
she jumps down to the floor
& moves past junior
she moves out of sight

junior gets up & walks
past me
he turns around & goes
to the foot of the armrest
of the loveseat & settles

9 26 03

kazan's obit

a door closed, & the talking
has ceased — midnight.
today, i read pritchard on frost
at the silver spoon & ate oatmeal
with sliced banana & nonfat milk.
then, i sat with an elderly sitcom
writer, a pilot & 2 men who sell
expensive cars.
the sitcom writer talked & talked
about kazan being a "rat fink
bastard" — how kazan had ruined
many lives.
kazan had died yesterday at age 94.
i talked about what a great stage
& film director kazan was — how
much i loved "america, america."
the sitcom writer compared kazan
to benedict arnold.

the only film the sitcom writer
ever liked was "the bicycle thief."

i stood up for the things i liked
& i was happiest when joe turkel,
an actor who acted in 3 kubrick
films: "the killing," "paths of
glory" & "the shining," sat down.
joe & i are each in 2 films listed
in the library of congress's
national film registry.
he's in "paths of glory" & "blade runner."
i'm in "mean streets" & "taxi driver."

joe said, "i would have liked to live
in 4 previous times of history:
when the dinosaurs were alive;
revolutionary america, when the declaration
of independence was signed; the time
of jesus; & munich 1920."

"why munich 1920?"
"so i could have killed hitler."

joe thinks kubrick is the greatest
film director ever.
"there is not a week goes by that
i don't think of stanley," he said.

he has a sense of art & i like him for
that. "paths of glory" is one of the 2 best
anti-war films ever made. joe was
also in "the sand pebbles." he made his
film debut in "city across the river" (1949).

9 30 03

i turn to movies & poetry

jonathan demme's assistant called
& said "we just finished shooting
a scene on a train in queens
& as we stepped off, jonathan said
to call you & tell you that he's
looking forward to working with you
next month."
"oh, that's nice. well, i'm looking
forward to working with jonathan, too.
i love his movies."
"we sent you blue pages for your
scene."
"thank you very much."

later, i went to citibank
& withdrew $50, mailed 15 flyers
for a poetry reading i'm doing
in 3 weeks. walked to 99¢ store.

i read a john kerry vietnam speech
& several chapters from saint luke
out loud.

i sat down & wrote a poem
to my sister who turned 77
last week.

baseball & blues on tv.
last night, i went to the jazz
bakery where i met bob dorough
before he appeared with dave
frishberg.
two poets on stage. two pianos.
two poets front row left. later right.

10 2 03

window closed

in a room with 4 cats
1 across the room
she jumped down from the brown
chair & went into the kitchen
1 sleeps on the black chest
1 on either side of me
on the brown sofa

the old male cat stays in
most of the time
the mother cat loves to eat
the chicken, turkey & fish we eat
the 2 young cats can't wait
to go out in the morning

i am always glad when all 4 cats
are in

10 3 03

mariposa avenue

mariposa avenue is always there
i look out our bedroom window
& see a tall palm tree, cars parked,
houses on each side
at times, i see a group of young
armenian men standing around a car
i hear young filipinos laughing as
they sit on & stand near a porch
i look down the street — mariposa
we live in the 3rd house on the east
side of mariposa
south of fountain
a hooker tried to drive over a cop
& was shot & killed on mariposa
a filipino gang used to hang out on
mariposa
a young armenian woman arrived
in a white limousine & celebrated
her wedding on mariposa
ramona grade school is at the north
west corner of mariposa avenue &
santa monica boulevard
armenians, peruvians, blacks, whites,
filipinos, poets, koreans, hispanics,…
live on either side of mariposa
it is always there when i look out
the window

10 7 03

meetings

i first met dick miller
in may 1975 in griffith park
when we acted together
in "crazy mama," dir. by j. demme

i first met don calfa
in summer stock, lake whalom
playhouse, fitchburg, mass.
in june 1962

i first met jon voight
in may 1970
at warner brothers
when i auditioned for & got
the role of parker in
"the all-american boy," written &
directed by charles eastman

i met harvey keitel, bill bush,
lane smith, victor argo, murray
moston, chris jones, larry dove,
alexandria holland, hector elizondo,
don nation, bill moor, lee hickman
in frank corsaro's acting class
in manhattan in the early-mid-
sixties

i met gene borkan, john aprea,
warren miller, al maines, tony
king, kip, henry jaglom
in the old world restaurant
on sunset blvd from 1968 to 1970

i met jonathan demme at
carmen argenziano's apartment
in west hollywood in 1975

i met jonathan kaplan in 1978
when i auditioned for (5 auditions)
& got the role of sgt. doberman
in "over the edge"

i met martin scorsese in 1967 in
a 42nd st office when i auditioned
for & got the role of the rapist
in his first feature, "who's that
knocking at my door?"

i fell in love with holly prado's
writing when i read her book *feasts*
& her writing drew me to her

10 11 03

the heat

books & movies have made
a difference in my life

baseball & poetry have
enriched my heaven

cats have warmed my heart
walking has opened my eyes

a young woman with a tattoo
on her lower back
rakes a small rectangle
of earth
in front of her small house on fountain

dozens of black birds gather
expecting rain
the funeral service was in spanish
except for "amazing grace"
& sections of the *bible* read
by her brother & 3 others

my wife has cared for me
in my frailties
& that has made all the difference

10 12 03

Meetings

I met Allen Ginsberg in a cab on St. Mark's Place. I had hailed a cab after Frank Corsaro's acting class had finished one night in early 1967 & as soon as I had gotten into the cab & out of the rain, a man knocked on the window & asked if I would mind sharing the cab. I said no. He got in with another man. I recognized Allen Ginsberg & introduced myself. I had recently sent him *amarillo born,* my first book, & he had replied with a postcard & said some nice things about my poetry. I kept the postcard on my wall for many years until 2002, when I packaged it for UCSD, La Jolla, when my papers were purchased to be in the Mandeville Special Collections Library. The cabbie took Allen to his place on the lower east side, he dropped the other man, a lawyer, off on the upper east side & took me home to 77th & Columbus.

I met Allen Ginsberg again in 1969 at the Old World Restaurant on the Strip. I was working as a waiter. "Are things beginning to break for you?" he asked. He was with Timothy Leary.

I met Ginsberg in Sept. 1987, in Lawrence, Kansas. I was playing Governor Delitt in the film, "Kansas," & I was staying in the same motel where Ginsberg, Creeley, & other poets, who were participating in a week-long poetry celebration, were staying. My son, Dylan, was with me & we met Allen in a hallway. Later, at breakfast, I heard Allen, who was giving an interview, say, "Poetry is speech that has eloquence." He was a fountain.

10 14 03

Meetings

I met Duffy in the early-mid-fifties on the baseball field at Sioux Ordnance Depot. He was an enthusiastic, roly-poly, baseball nut. He lived on the base because his father was an officer. He wasn't as good a player as we were, but he loved the game. We lived in Ordville, the housing project for civilian workers. We climbed over the fence to play on the field. One rainy day we wanted to play a game & we didn't have a ball. Duffy had a baseball signed by Robin Roberts. We asked him if we could use it. He didn't want to play with it. Duffy wanted to belong so much that we talked him into letting us use the ball. He played on one side. We threw & hit & caught the ball & threw it & after an hour or so the ball was soggy & ruined & Duffy was sad that he had let us use his baseball autographed by Robin Roberts.

10 14 03

Meetings

I met my first wife, Rita Ann Solomon, in 1966. In the 5 years that I lived in New York City, I threw only 1 party. I was living in a 3-1/2 room apartment, fifth floor walk-up, on 25th & Tenth. Harvey Keitel came. He was in my acting class. He brought Rita & Michele, both from Brooklyn where he was from. Lane Smith & Victor Argo, fellow acting students came. Frank Corsaro, our esteemed teacher, was there. The fellow who lived next door, Mike Pavao, an art student who studied with Barnett Newman, brought his girlfriend, Bette Midler. She sang. He played his banjo. Lee Hickman, who turned me on to poetry & was also in Frank's acting class, was there. He sat quietly & observed. Rita & I began going together after that party & we married the following year. She was a beautiful young woman & a superb artist.

10 17 03

naming the hood

3:36 a.m. & i can't sleep
third time i've gotten up tonight
have read hemingway's letters
& pritchard on frost

pal joey sits in my lap
rose sleeps on the sofa
junior sleeps by the loveseat
egypt, in the foyer, in repose

success defines itself
by going deep into the soul,
the imagination, a reality
beyond stardom, money, fame

where humility resides in
a heart as big as dodger stadium
a stillness greater than
the absence of police helicopters

where mystery measures not
the rising price of a house
a lowering of mortgage interest rates
where movement chases sorrow

not by shopping, not by tv, not
by how fast one devours
the latest restaurant's signature
dish, nor speeds to relay
a cognitive car in a freeway circuit

nor creates
without humbling
the necessary closeness
of a faraway sky star

in its transient closeness
in a nonbelief prophecy
in baseball as religion
in a secular heart

where light travels to define
appetite, devouring commerce
to define the hurriedness
of a one-way no return beauty
only miles away with no reservation
till we meet in between
the arrivals & departures
until the sounds of planes & cars
return us to our missing
ragged scratch along the rectangle

10 21 03

plans

today, i received a call from betsy,
production coordinator, "the manchurian
candidate," asking me if i would be
willing to fly to new york city on
tues., nov. 18th, have a costume fitting
on wed., nov. 19th, & work early the
following week. "yes."

obviously, working on the movie
is the main thing, but i would
like to walk around midtown;
eat healthy food — grilled fish &
chicken & vegetables; see & hear toni
morrison read from *love* at a black
church in brooklyn, thur. night; go
to the metropolitan art museum & see
the el greco show; go to the guggen-
heim for the rosenquist retrospective;
take a bus down fifth avenue to
washington square; walk through
the village; check out some of the
places i used to live; eat at felida,
243 east 58th: "pastas as thick &
homey as sunday supper at mamma's
house — will leave you warm, satis-
fied ..."; walk through the theatre
district & 42nd st; visit with michele
& shelley, frank corsaro, jonathan
cott, victor argo.

and continue doing what i do every day
now: read out loud a john kerry speech,
read out loud from the *bible,* work on my
scene, observe kerry, & other congressmen
& women on tv. be mindful.

buy the *new york times* & read it. walk
in central park. walk by the park
wald (58th & sixth), frank corsaro's acting
class — 54th, between sixth & seventh,

cort hotel, 48th & eighth — places i lived
& studied in.

take the subway to battery park &
ride the staten island ferry, or maybe
not, since i might get seasick.

visit the public library at 42nd & fifth,
where i read many plays, theatre criticism
& theatre history.

maybe even catch some jazz.

10 23 03

tuesday

two weeks from today, i go to new york
city to act in "the manchurian candidate."
i have, daily, read out loud a 5 or 6
page speech by john kerry, to learn
about his concerns & vision, to practice
a political speech, & i have also, daily,
read out loud from the *bible* to strength-
en my voice & my soul.
i am in one, 4-page scene with meryl
streep. i play congressman flores.
i have chosen to be cleaning my
reading glasses before & during my
lines.
my second & third choices include
more conventional, out-going gestures.
i walk down fountain, sunset, holly-
wood, mariposa, normandie, vermont
saying my lines — loud, soft, varied.

limousine, first class airplane ticket,
parker meridien, $100 a day per diem,
$4,000 a week. one week contract.

the day after arriving in manhattan,
i have a costume fitting. then 4
days off, shoot mon. & tues., fly
home wed., nov. 26th.
i have made reservations for holly
& me to eat thanksgiving dinner
at edendale grill, at 6 p.m., on thur., 11-27.

11 04 03

a warmth

she has her front paws
crossed in front of her

her body next to mine
on the brown couch

she's gray & white
tender & relaxed & warm

in the night
a night of rain

a night with the heat on
outside a dog yelps

another dog barks
the cats wake & listen

an occasional car drives by
on mariposa or fountain

the cats lower their heads
& go back to sleep

the young gray & white female
rests her body next to mine

when i first got up at 4 a.m.
she & the old male came to me

11 16 03

tuesday

today i got up at 7 a.m.
drank juice, coffee,
bathed, ate shredded wheat,
brushed junior twice,
gave joey & rose some pets

packed my toilet kit & duffel bag
kissed my wife twice
at 9:40 i looked outside to see
if the limousine was there
it was
the driver carried my suitcase

he took the city streets to lax
an attendant checked me in
electronic ticket
now i sit in the admiral's lounge
it's quiet
free food & drinks
a nice, clear view of planes & sky
half an hour wait till boarding

12:15 — first class, 2b, aisle seat,
american airlines flight #4
to new york, jfk

11 18 03

admiral's lounge lax

demme has hired me
to act in movies
in marysville, ca. ("citizens band,"
3 weeks)
in fayetteville, ark. ("fighting
mad," 6 weeks)
in pittsburgh, pa. ("the silence
of the lambs," 1 week)
in philadelphia, pa. ("philadelphia,"
3 weeks, 2 days)
in philadelphia, pa. ("beloved,"
1 week)
in new york city, n.y. ("the
manchurian candidate," 1 week)
in l.a., ca. ("crazy mama," 3
days & "swing shift," 3 days)
he also hired me to act
in 2 commercials, "people for
the american way," produced
by norman lear

i met him in june at paramount
to talk about "the manchurian
candidate"
5 months later, i am getting ready
to fly first class to n.y.c. to work
in "the manchurian candidate"

11 18 03

plane trip

had a nice trip
ate grilled chicken
with sweet potatoes & asparagus
chocolate brownie cheesecake
lowfat milk — 2 bottles of water
read joyce johnson's & kerouac's
letters, watched "a world apart"
on dvd — personal video — enjoyable
talked a little bit to the woman
next to me — works for american
airlines & has an upholstery business
she met her girlfriend from dallas
& they spent 4 days in l.a.

had to wait a little bit for my bag
cold when i hit the outside
friendly chat with the town car
driver — a yankee fan, his son
likes the mets & looks like piazza

he pointed out the 59th st bridge
we came over the tri-boro bridge
manhattan is huge, bunched
together
my room has a study area,
living room, bedroom, bathroom

maggie, 2nd a.d. called,
i have a 1:30 p.m. p.u.
for a wardrobe fitting
will be picked up on 56th st side

i went to a corner deli
& got a tuna, with tomato & lettuce,
on whole wheat
small milk & lukewarm water
the counterman wouldn't give me
ice cubes — wanted me to buy
bottled water

went to a store on sixth
bought an orange & 6 small cans
of prune juice
came home, ate the orange
& watched gore vidal trash
the u.s.a. on charlie rose

slept a couple of hours
got up & checked the new script
no changes for me

11 19 03

wed. (parker meridien)

got up at 9 a.m.
had gotten up several times
during the night

went downstairs for breakfast
after i had drunk 2 small cans
of prune juice
& washed up

ate oatmeal with pears
& low fat milk
& 3 cups of coffee
read the *n.y. times*

many businessmen
many young businesswomen

waiters & busboys friendly
& quick
seeing them work
reminded me of when
i was studying acting in n.y.
from 1963–1968
i worked as a waiter & counterman
i was also clean, friendly & quick

11 19 03

manhattan

o, the buildings are so tall
i get dizzy looking upward
people walk against the light
cops stand & watch
stands with hot dogs, pretzels, chestnuts, . . .
yellow cabs by the hundreds
many delis
dry cleaning stores
clothing stores, coffee shops
pizza joints, new york memoribilia

men in burberry coats,
young hopefuls

today, i walked by the stage deli,
past carnegie hall
i studied acting with strasberg
in the building at 56th & 7th ave.

saw the park
from central park south & 6th ave.
carriages & horses went by

i walked by the now gone park wald hotel
58th west of 6th ave., where i lived
past where corsaro taught acting
on 54th st., between 6th & 7th avenues
invigorating
cool & crisp after a morning rain

11 19 03

in my hotel room

i feel lucky to be in new york
staying in a hotel on 56th, between
6th & 7th avenues
getting $100 a day per diem
a good wage
& most importantly, to be working
in a good film with a great
director, who has cared for me
over the years

it's a dream fulfilled
to be working in a movie in manhattan

11 19 03

a date in n.y.c. with a hometown girl

i can't sleep
i look out the bedroom window
& it's still raining

when i was living at the park wald
hotel, 58th, just west of 6th avenue,
i was studying acting & working
as a waiter

there was a woman from my hometown
who was an airline attendant
her name was diane & she worked
for braniff
she had been a year behind me in school
& we had dated a few times

i enlisted in the navy & when i went
to college after completing my tour
of duty, we began to correspond
i was going to nebr. state college,
at kearney & she was attending
southern methodist university
her letters always smelled of perfume

i wrote diane from the park wald
& we decided to go out on a date again
in new york city
when she flew in on braniff
on vacation

i got us orchestra tickets
for "what makes sammy run?"
starring steve lawrence
we ate at a seafood restaurant
before the broadway play
i wore a brown, 3-piece, tweed suit
that i had had tailor made

after the play, we walked back
to the park wald — i had gotten her
a room next to mine

she said she was tired & she wanted
to go to her room & sleep
& she would see me in the morning

the next morning, i knocked on her door
& there was no answer
i asked the clerk if he had seen her
& he said she had checked out in the
middle of the night

it's raining out now & i never knew why

11 20 03

the bus past toledo

i took the bus up madison avenue
got off & walked west to the metro-
politan art museum
to see the el greco show
$7 — senior citizen
checked my jacket & umbrella

a magnificent inner spirit
religious scenes & figures
a well, a fountain, a mirror,...
miracles, faith, saints, jesus,
mary, saint peter, saint francis,
saint paul
jesus driving the money lenders
from the temple

a great rising of spirit
just tremendous biblical representa-
tion, so alive
just lifts the soul, heart, breath
divine rain
makes all the leaves in central
park turn green, orange, red
& fall into post-impressionist's hay
stacks &
picasso heralds el greco as pre-cubist
with dancing & naked religious figures
prophesying picasso's dancing ladies
a shore of wonder
bathing in the giving over of the
personal for inner biblical realism

the traffic, stopped for some reason
traffic backed up from central
park south up to 90th

white figures, horses & carriages, men
with cameras, a television crew
the sun came out
el greco of crete lifted up our hearts

above the commerce & the tv & the
arrests of celebrities & gossip & fast city
he lifted up the child & the god undenying
breath of the naked body in heaven
just lifted up

11 20 03

Meetings: A New

Shelly said, "See those two people over there with the telescope. They have it pointed east toward the top of those buildings where falcons fly & nest." We were standing on the east side of the lake in Central Park. The two men & the telescope were across the lake from us. I had met Shelly at his apartment at 40 E. 89th St. & after visiting his wife, Michele, at her job a few blocks from their home, Shelly & I walked to Fifth Ave. by the Metropolitan Art Museum, then entered Central Park & walked to Central Park South. We sat on a bench along the way & talked about Ginsberg — Shelly is reading a bio on Ginsberg — we talked about the Dalai Lama — Shelly has seen him in the park twice, recently — we discussed our wives, poetry, yoga, friends. We sat in the sun & listened.

11 21 03

meetings

victor argo has cancer
he's playing santiago
in "anna in the tropics,"
his first broadway play

i am in new york city
working in the film,
"the manchurian candidate"
& victor called me last night

& said, "there will be a ticket
for you at the box office
tomorrow for the 2 p.m. show"

his character had an arc
he was like his factory's
new cigar, "glorioso, perfecto"

he told me to come backstage
afterward
i praised his work
he talked to the director

we walked up 8th to a puerto
rican restaurant & ate pork,
with black beans & yellow rice

"i'm not afraid of dyin'
i've done everything
i wanted to do:
i wanted to drink, i drank
i wanted to smoke pot, i smoked pot
i wanted to get laid, i got laid
i wanted to act, i acted"

"tomorrow, i go for chemotherapy
a 6-hour treatment once
every 3 weeks"
he pointed to his middle chest
"if they can shrink it
the chances are good

that they can remove it,
if not, the chances
are not good
but i've got the best doctors
there are, at n.y.u.
the procedure is costing
a million dollars
i'll lose my hair in 6 days"

we discussed fellow actors
we knew: harvey keitel,
lane smith, don nation, nick padula
we talked about movies
we've been in: his favorite
jarmusch film is "dead man"
victor was in "ghost dog,"
dir. by jarmusch

we talked about our acting
careers & our pensions
we talked about n.y.c. restaurants
he eats out a lot
doesn't worry about money
because of his s.a.g. pension,
work & residuals
he's also a good cook

before we got back to 45th,
where the royale theatre is,
he bought a newspaper, a
soda & a piece of cake

he said he would read the paper,
rest a while & then do 15 minutes
of yoga before the 30-minute
call for the 8 p.m. performance
we hugged, "my prayers are with
you; i wish you the best," i said

11 22 03
(died 4-6-04, age 69)

cort hotel

i just stared at the building
at 48th & 8th, nw corner
when i first came to new york
to study acting, i stayed at the cort
hotel
i paid $16 a week for a bed & a sink
the toilet, with shower, was off the hallway
later, i paid $19 for a similar situation
i lived there for over a year
it was above a bar the play pen
a lonely time, an exciting time
seeking acting work, studying acting,
working as a waiter, eating
steaks at jim downey's, in my room
reading plays that i had checked out
from the 42nd st library

i had just left victor
he went back to the royale theatre
i was walking back to the parker
meridien
the sidewalk was filled with people
5:45 p.m., saturday
i looked at the building from several
perspectives
looked at its shape, the windows
i had stared out of
i couldn't tell what its use was now
it looked like people lived there
it didn't seem like it was a hotel
the streets were much more crowded now

11 23 03

central park, warm visit & quiet

michele made us breakfast
i had oat bran & coffee
shelly, michele & i walked on 89th
past the guggenheim into the park
we walked around the reservoir
i enjoyed looking at the skyline,
the water & the sunlight on the
water & the changing colors of the
leaves

we walked to central park west
down c.p.w. to 81st, over to
columbus, past 79th where i
stayed at june bassett's apartment,
5b, at 79th & columbus, sw corner,
when i did "taxi driver," down
columbus to 370 columbus, between
77th & 78th, where i lived with
rita when we first got married,
1-bedroom apt. in a building with
an elevator, $72 a month

the building looked the same
the lobby also seemed the same
maybe a different paint job

we walked a few more blocks
we talked, said our goodbyes
i caught a bus down columbus
to 57th st., got off, walked
east on 57th, past 333 w. 57th
where marina jessup, a fellow
acting student, had a large single
with kitchen & bathroom

home to my hotel
a hotel is a city unto itself
i read a kerry speech out loud
practiced my scene

i got overwhelmed, the other evening,
by all the people in the times square
area & today there were so many
people on columbus avenue in
the 70s

the hotel room is quiet

11 23 03

11 24 03

i'm dressed in a 3 piece, charcoal gray
ermenegildo zegna suit
i sit in my room on 36th st
by the jacob k. javitz center
waiting for the first shot to be lit

we rehearsed several times
meryl streep is the main one in this scene
she plays eleanor
roger corman, obba babatunde, walter
mosley are also in the scene

jonathan was happy to see me
i said hi to tak

had nice talks with obba & roger c.
this morning
we are all staying at the parker meridien
roger's favorite directors are
eisenstein & howard hawks
i talked briefly with w. mosley
he said he was born in watts
grew up near pico & fairfax
& now lives in the village
goes back to l.a. 8, 9 times a year

it's starting to warm up a little

11 24 03

flight home day

12:15, saw roger corman come in
to the parker meridien
"it was an honor to work with you, roger,
& talk with you; you're one of the best."
"good to see you, harry."
he went to the elevator
i continued to wait for a town car,
bls, to take to kennedy.

when i thanked jonathan demme last
night after i wrapped
he said, "great stuff, harry,
give my best to holly & dylan."

last night, i got to the hotel at 7:10,
walked to sardi's, ate crab cakes & salad,
came back to the hotel, called holly &
told her i completed the acting job, "it
went well. i'll see you tomorrow
about 7. we'll eat at edendale grill
for thanksgiving. i love you."

this morning, i got up at 7, had juice
& coffee, read the *n.y. times,* ate eggs
& potatoes at the park cafe, walked
to central park south, right to fifth,
past the plaza down to 57th,
right to the parker meridian.

got my money, keys, earrings from
tiffany's in a mint-colored box & bag
from the safe.

i sit at kennedy, 1:40 p.m.
at 1:45, take a motion sickness pill
board at 2, depart at 2:30
arrive lax at 5:32.

i'm glad to have worked,
glad it went well
got an extra scene.

had a great meal mon. night
at keen's steak house, 72 w. 36th st
between 5th & 6th avenues
with j. demme, roger & julie corman,
kristi zea, carol littleton, walter
mosley, daniel pyne, the writer,
among others — demme paid.
i'm happy to be going home.

11 26 03

Meetings

Several years ago, Cahuenga Press published Jonathan Cott's book of poetry, *Homelands.* I edited it & worked very closely with Jonathan on the phone for a few months. Yesterday, we finally met in person. Jonathan Demme sent a car for him & he came to the Jacob K. Javitz Center where we were shooting "The Manchurian Candidate." Cott saw some of the scene I was in, on the monitor. We broke for lunch & went to a nearby place on 36th street where the catering was. Polly, Jonathan's assistant, brought J. Cott up to me. We were both happy to see each other for the first time. We stood in line & got our meals. He is a vegeterian & got the vegetable lasagna. I chose chicken, squash & spinach. I took him to a table, pulled out a chair for him next to Walter Mosley. Across from Walter, sat Roger Corman. Next to Roger was his wife, Julie. J. Demme sat down next to Julie. I introduced J. Cott to Roger, Julie & Walter. Jonathan Cott & I talked mostly to each other. "You're a wonderful writer. It was an honor for Cahuenga Press to have published *Homelands.*" "Well, it's an honor for me," he said. He said he loved the Ann Stanford book. I told him about the great, full page review it got in the *L. A. Times* Sunday Book Review. He asked how Holly's back was. He asked about her poetry. I told him that Cahuenga Press was publishing her selected poems & prose (425 pages) next spring. "What's the title?" *"These Mirrors Prove It."* "Wow, that's great! Is it from a title of one of her other books?" "I think it's a line or phrase from one of her poems." We talked about his writing — he's working on a book about memory. He's had shock treatments, so it's difficult for him to remember some things. He can remember childhood things very well. We talked about Phoebe MacAdams, Lewis MacAdams, Joe Brainard's writing, El Greco at the Metropolitan Art Museum, *Rolling Stone,* Jann Wenner, Aram & Gailyn Saroyan, Demme's music videos, his work in London for *Rolling Stone* — "Jonathan Demme & I were both in London at the same time, though we didn't know each other," Jackie O. — she edited 4 of Cott's books, his apartment, his health, my stay in New York, his book: *The Search For Omm Sety,* my poetry, Harry Smith, Lafcadio Hearn, Glenn Gould, . . . I only ate half of my meal because we talked so much. Soon, it was time to go back to the set. On the way back, I put my arm around Roger Corman's shoulder, "Jonathan just said 'I can't believe it's Roger Corman,'" I said. Roger smiled. They talked. On the set, Jonathan Cott sat in a director's chair. "I'm glad we met," I said, "I love your writing. Give me a hug." We hugged, I went to work.

11 26 03

Red Snow Fence

12-31-03 to 7-27-04

Actualities

Wedding Reaffirmation

It's 4:09 a.m. on the last day of the year. On Sat., Dec. 27th, 2003, at 2:30 p.m., Holly & I arrived at the home of Dick & Lainie Miller in Toluca Lake to celebrate Dick's 75th birthday (Dec. 25th) & to witness the reaffirmation of Dick & Lainie's marriage in a wedding ceremony performed by their daughter, Barbara. Barbara & her daughter, Autumn, age 13, welcomed us. They were very gracious & warm & dressed elegantly. Dick appeared. He was happy & handsome. He wore a perfectly tailored black tuxedo with a white tie. More guests arrived, including actor Robert Forster, John Regis, producer-writer Ira Behr, film director Joe Dante, producer-writer Fred Rappaport, actor Jonathan Haze, actor Mel Welles . . . There were about 25–30 people in attendance, all connected to the film & tv industries, all friends, co-workers & fans of Dick & Lainie. The event was filmed. Lainie was beautiful. She wore a gorgeous, creme-colored dress. Barbara did a superb job of performing the wedding reaffirming vows. Dick & Lainie kissed twice. Warm & beautiful. Champagne was served. Roast beef, turkey, cole slaw ... were in the kitchen. Ira said, "Come on, Harry, let's get some food." "I'll follow the producer." I made myself a half of a roast beef sandwich on rye bread with mustard, with cole slaw. Later, a delicious strawberry cake (2 tiers, $75) was served with coffee. At one point, Ira, who was talking with Fred Rappaport, called me over, "Harry, we were quoting your lines from 'Taxi Driver,' when you tried to sell Robert De Niro a piece of Errol Flynn's bathtub. Tell Fred how that scene came about." I told Fred about getting the idea & telling Scorsese about it & how much Marty loved it. I told him the lines & how the scene was shot. That's how the party was. We were there to celebrate Dick & Lainie's wedding & its reaffirmation, but we also talked to each other about acting, movies & tv, in front of & behind the camera. There were 4 actors, Dick, Jonathan, Mel & Jackie Joseph, who had acted in the cult film, "The Little Shop of Horrors" (1960), dir. by Roger Corman. Joe Dante had hired Dick to act in many of his films. Ira had hired Dick to act in his tv series, "Fame." Dick & I had acted in "Karen Sisco," a tv series that Robert Forster starred in. Everyone was kind & friendly. Holly & I enjoyed talking to Dick, Lainie, Barbara, Autumn, Robert F., John R., Ira B., Fred R., Jonathan H., among others. A delightful day. As we were getting ready to leave, I said goodbye to Fred Rappaport. He said, "I also liked you in 'Handle With Care.'" We thanked Dick & Lainie. Said goodbye to them & their daughter & granddaughter. A lovely affair.

12 31 03

Time

For all time Jesus
For some time moon
For eternity Emily
For ages Julia
For walks & memories Hometown
For welts & acorns Friendship
For wakenings Jealousy snaps
For hunger Brother
For long term shoulder Screenwriter
For blessing & heart Pension
For absence Venal Friend
For sacred kiss Widow
For all time Hawthorne
For tunnel & tv Commercials
For sacred trust Film Director
For hope & resurrection Candle
For briefness Love & War
For U.S. honor afar Marines
For sustaining Work
For bridge & memory Hometown Friend
For time lost Baseball
For comfort Cat

1 2 04

paul brooks died 8 days ago

paul wrote me a letter
from county jail
asking me why
hadn't i visited him lately
he needed books to read
& money
he signed it "your venal friend,
paul brooks"
after visiting him at county
& giving him what he had asked for
i left
turned & looked at him
he had a smile on his face
like he could survive anywhere

i wanted to blow up that place
as i was leaving

i visited paul at county hospital
in east l.a. when he had a leg operation
after he'd been hit by a motorcycle

i visited paul at torrance general
hospital
i took him to ucla, to st. john's,
to a clinic

we met at beyond baroque
in the wed. night poetry workshop
he saw ann christie walk in
to the workshop — she was young
& pretty with large breasts — &
he wrote her a love poem
tore it out of his notebook
& gave it to her

he wrote love poems & poems
of anger
he wrote excellent jail poems

i took him to ralphs, to rite aid,
to pharmacies, to hardware stores,
to radio shack

a machine breathed him last year
for 10 days
he pulled through & lived another
year

he was a poet, a father, a husband,
a foster child, a brother, a reader
of w.h. auden & sci-fi & philosophy &
the *l.a. times* & the *new york times*, a
library book thief, a friend

he lived with his wife, barb, in a camper shell
he lived with barb & sean in the ellison
paloma & speedway

1 17 04

venice poet

equally at home
with an iron & a pen

he would sit at a
brown rectangular table
type his poems fast
draw short quick
visible breaths

he owned 3 vehicles
at once

he had left many tens,
twenties, fives on a table
said "take some"

he liked to watch
pro football on tv

a teacher at lacc said
"paul had so much energy
it was like he had wires
coming out of his head"

the last time he saw his son
his son kicked paul in the shins
paul said, "it's his way
of saying he loves me"

he switched channels
back & forth
between "s.w.a.t."
& "police woman"

he had trouble
breathing, he was
in the hospital —
he asked me to get him
a double espresso

he knew auden's
"there will be no peace"
by heart

he had a bum leg
& a beard

nomenclature & status quo
were words in his poems

he was anti-religious
& anti-bush

paul sat at his desk
by a window
looked out at paloma

he liked the poet bob
kaufman

1 17 04

night word

i read to sleep
i read with egypt in my lap
my left hand on her left side
a wedding ring, gold, on
white leg & gray body

i read at 12:40 a.m.
in the living room with 3 cats
i read john gardner's essay
on *bartleby:* "ah, bartleby!
ah, humanity!"

i read *the collected poems*
of frank o'hara
i read to learn
i write in shadow

each night i go to sleep
with my wife at 10:30 p.m.
usually i wake in the middle
of the night, get my robe
& slippers on, grab my reading
glasses & open the bedroom
door, close it, get a book, read

i read shadow i read light
the room warms
lately, i have read *bellow, a*
biography, by james atlas
i have read 500 of hemingway's
letters

i return to the shore
of my mother's & sister's comfort
when they sat next to me
read to me & i learned to read
along the road to san gabriel
& mountain home & denver

i read books from the bookmobile
& i read in the country schoolhouse

there is a stillness to the word
i read each word
the word has always been before me
i follow the word

1 18 04

january

we were eating shrimp
pesto risotto & vibrant salad
& i said i wish i could
remember deutsch's blackboard
info on metaphor & simile
& i could write a poem explaining
each

& she said isn't the only difference
between them is the use of the word
like?

i cut up 1 shrimp on a small paper plate
divided the pieces into 2
put 1/2 on another paper plate

placed them on the floor
for 2 of our 4 eats
the old male did not eat his
the mother cat ate both
sat near us wanting more

1 18 04

welcome

the friends are all friends
in hollywood
when they want you to be
part of their audience

he sat down & read out loud
the words of "tangerine"
i thought of chet baker
& told him so

the young female cat
was shy & stayed in the drain pipe
earlier the sanding noise
made me sick
& i told him so

when i was young
i knew all the statistics
now, i read at night
& pet the cats

chernobyl, ghana & staten island
are never far from my dreams

father & ritual, doctor & heart,
women & freedom
do not send me back

2 2 04

window wired

i would pet my cat
as i practiced my lines
& speak in a quiet love
as if i were peeling an orange

a language lost to politics
an actual caring for the poor

i heard a plane
& a woman rising

where is our love
if not in the handing
& offering

i saw her as another woman
in front of a fundamental church
on olympic
on the way to help
a bereft schizophrenic

the pages still held together
kabala bop among an old building
its poems wrapped around
by the seaside
what no longer resides
ashes fervent in love

2 2 04

Hero

For the firstborn
For love
For war
For marriage
For college & work
For being an FBI agent
For fatherhood
For aloneness in secrecy
For family
For loving one woman
For being smart & handsome
For capturing a killer
For being a foreign language
expert
For capturing a spy

For being on an oil tanker
in Pearl Harbor, Dec. 7, 1941
when it was bombed
For surviving

For learning & listening
For going out & returning
For progeny
For two sons
For grandchildren

For wife & sons' wives
For Hero Beauty

2 9 04

early february

"you're just a pretty little girl,
little egypt."
"we were visiting auntie in denver
& we went out to eat
& she said she didn't care where we ate
but she didn't want to eat at a seafood
place.
then, at the restaurant we went to,
she ordered seafood.
and then while we were eating,
she would look at each of our entrees
& say, 'i should have ordered that.'"
"you know how we lived in ordville —
in those cinder block apartments,
with a shower & no bathtub — so,
whenever we went to auntie's, it
seemed like she lived so elegantly:
that long maroon sofa in her big
living room, a large bathroom with
a tub, she had a big bedroom with
a king size bed & in the kitchen where
she kept snails in a glass container,
& the porch, with a bed, that had a
view of east high. denver was mecca
to us. growing up in a little town
in nebr."
"when uncle kirt would get mad at
auntie, he would go sleep in the bed
in the porch."
"i remember once we ate in the cafe
downstairs where auntie worked
as a cashier & daddy ordered a california
burger, you know, a hamburger with
lettuce & tomato & afterward daddy
said, 'that tasted like sawdust.'"
a siren outside. 1:42 a.m.
three cats sleep on a green blanket
on the sofa. egypt sleeps in my lap.
georgie said, "on feb, 26th, markey

& i will celebrate our 61st wedding
anniversary."
they were married in kansas.
her parents & our parents attended.
georgie & margaret met in grade school
began going together at age eighteen
married at age twenty.
margaret said, "harry, georgie & you
are my favorites."
we talked about grandma monk.
"she was the most gentle person
i ever met," i said,
"and mother. we had a good mother."
"she loved you, harry. she was very
protective of you," margaret said.
we talked about steve & donn & their
families. margaret asked about holly.
"she's a real nice woman," margaret
said.
"we've been together twenty-seven years,"
i said.
"you're so pretty, little egypt."
i rub her under her chin, down
her neck, scratch her back.
we talked about margaret's vertigo,
about my motion sickness. about the
academy of motion picture arts & sciences.
"it's an honor to belong," i said.
about donn's religiousness: "we want
to all be together in the next world,
he tells steve." about donn being the
head of a salvation army place in down-
town washington, d.c., that has 150 beds.
that helps homeless people, alcoholics,
drug addicts.
we talked about our family — the
different fields each of us worked in.
"you're the hero of the family, georgie.
you & margaret have a beautiful family."
"well, if i wasn't with georgie, i'd
want to be with you, harry."
"two of my favorite photographs are
one with georgie as a young man,
standing, with his first baseman's
mitt on, down by his left leg & the

other, you & georgie in the frame, georgie
in his navy dress blues. you used to keep
that photo on your tv, i believe. a
beautiful shot."
i rub egypt's nose.

2 9 04

past periphery

communion is important to me
i find it with my wife, my son,
my family, in writing poetry,
acting, reading poetry, watching
movies & with a few creative people

i realized today
that i cannot continue
to seek communion
with most friends, actors, poets
i cannot continue
to take them seriously in that way

communion requires depth,
mystery, respect, a listening to one
another

communion is rare
like religion, like light, like repose,
like friendship
like compassion
a heart to lay
one's light on
a light to lift one's fear
to be allowed to be heard
each actual word
to be given as grace
to look into darkness
as into light & not look away
from the forward center

2 18 04

kindness & occupation

the four gang guys' names
are chaos, rain, indian, owl

it rains for four days & nights
nineteen friends & strangers

sat in a library room
remembering a poet

paul ironed clothes in remembrance
paul drew short visible breaths

short declarative sentences are
not enough to declare

a foster child, a sailor, a library book thief
an existential wolf

lived on berendo, on lexington, paloma
whose body burned, whose breath waited

to catch a boy & his sister left
at a foster home placement center

waited for his mother who gave him a dime
& said she'd be back in a little while

waited for the pretty woman he wrote
poems to, to reveal the muse inside himself

2 23 04

the printed word

i record to say yes
to life to what actually
took place: when, where,
who
why, because it is a life
a man who acted
who learned the words
who repeated, who found
a soul in syntax
who listened
who had a passion
who learned from his
acting teacher
who read plays
from the college library
from the public library
at 42nd & 5th
who dreamed of love
who rode greyhounds
from a small town
in western nebraska
to new york city

who painted flats
who gathered props
who built sets
who tore down sets

who read theatre criticism
who saw play after play
who did scene after scene
who sought acting work
in manhattan, in hollywood
who was hired by guy palmerton,
scorsese, corman, kaplan,
schrader, demme

who worked for warner brothers,
sony, mgm, twentieth century fox,
universal, paramount

who broke down & wept
in virgin megastore
seeing his name listed
in film, tv, video books

who wept on sunset & laurel,
an unknown, working
& not working actor

who receives a s.a.g. pension,
residuals, who did 2 acting
jobs last year, 5 the year
before

whose heart breaks in
gratitude each time he
thanks the lord for his
life as an actor
a modest living

3 9 04

The Reason Heart

the reason heart

each morning, i read
2 or 3 of hemingway's letters
at night, i read a chapter
or 2 of wineapple's *hawthorne*

when i began to study acting,
i bought all of hemingway's
books & read them in my hotel room,
on the subway, at a village cafe

& i bought & read
9 books on hemingway

as i grow older & the acting jobs
are fewer & fewer
& as i eat lunch with actors
who are older

& in 2 or 3 are there caring & comfort
& in most a desire to work, an uncaring
for films & directors i hold dear

& in hemingway was the theme
of continuing life with grace & dignity
even though physical damage &
damage to the psyche has taken place

& the spiritual pain has an inner,
indefinable reason to hope
& it is why i read & why i write

3 11 04

that's what we do

egypt crouches on top of the filing
cabinet.
junior lies on his left side
facing the french doors.
joey sleeps on the black chest,
rose on the love seat.

jim called today
i will fly to newark on fri., july 2nd,
wait for jim & mae to arrive
& then drive with them to our hotel.
sat., we eat at marie's at 4 p.m.
sun., there's a baseball game
at 6 p.m.
dinner & fireworks.
a celebration of bob & shio's 50th
wedding anniversary.
mon., i'll fly home.

today, i was reading *hawthorne,* by
brenda wineapple, at farmers market.
howie dayton, a 77-year-old actor
sat down at the table.
we talked about his first, new cell phone
he had just bought
& a new movie with jim carey
he had recently seen
& "captain newman, m.d.,"
a movie he had acted in
early in his career.

a couple he knew stopped by
howie introduced them to me.
the woman bent over to read
the title of my book, *"hawthorne,"*
she said, "i haven't read him since
high school."
howie said, "harry's an intellectual,
he even reads poetry."

junior walks around the living room
rose hops up onto the couch & climbs
into my lap.
i pet her behind her ears.
i fed her fresh roast turkey for
supper
while holly & i ate turkey sandwiches.

"feed her turkey & pet her behind
her ears when she comes home,"
the cat seer said.

3 13 04

for a poet dead

1.
paul brooks died january 9, 2004
of heart failure
in his sleep
in his apartment: #201, 15 paloma ave.,
venice, ca.

i raised $863 in two days
to pay for paul's burial
steve goldman & i have been working
together to bury paul
steve dealt with barbara, the funeral
parlors, made arrangements, filled
out forms ...

steve reads the forms to barbara
makes sure she understands them
before he asks her to sign

steve set up a memorial reading
for paul on sat., feb. 21st, 2004,
at the venice library
it's steve's reading series

barbara gets $874 a mo. from s.s.i.
her rent is $1,168
steve has suggested to her
that a board & care might be
a good place for her

2.
we visit a widow
i give her a copy
of her & paul's marriage record
from the temple of man

i look through his books:
patchen, auden, virgil

empty bottles of oxygen
in the living room

3.
a poet friend has been dead
two months
& i help his widow
with money for food & rent

his breathing was laconic
his poetry was more than the sum
of his stanzas
the empty oxygen tanks

his widow received the location
of his ashes in the riverside
national cemetery

it is 4:19 a.m.
& i find myself wide awake
a mild chill about my ankles
& bare legs

1 28 04 to 3 16 04
(paul brooks — 1939–2004)

prayer

thank you, lord, for breath,
bones, heart, lungs, stomach,
legs, arms, this body with skin
for eyes, nose, ears, touch,
with fingers, head, brain,
hair, all amazing sexual things
all sentient beings, thought
& seasons, beasts & sky
for clouds, books, seas, hills, roads,
presidents, armor, bill of rights,
for wife, son, mischief, record
player, radio, tv, phone, lp & cd
video & dvd
for continents & crosses, iron,
shields, car, moon, cat, horse, dog
for home, book, shelter, dinner
oatmeal, rock cornish game hen,
spinach souffle, sweet potato
for typewriter, typing paper, for
friend & friend's journey
for brothers, sister, dad & mom
for walk along sunset boulevard
for fog, sunshine, rain, rifle,
wagon, helicopter, skyscraper,
cock & cunt, breasts, tongue, taste
for journey unaltered
chimney, viaduct, sod house
indian, arrow & train
country schoolhouse, bed, bath

3 23 04

Red Snow Fence

the passing near

poetry, basketball, food
there is a settling in poetry
winning, looking down the road
to win, to gain home court advantage
to have the best record
to be aware of those things
but, to live in the moment

to be the first served
salmon, corn, spinach
fingerling potatoes
a slice of lemon-hazelnut cake

"poetry is all-embracing," she says
good poetry relaxes you
the truth told, real & precise

fictional, also
whitman was all-embracing in his poetry

there are those who are cruel
who do not succeed in their own minds
minds directed toward the external
& they sew discord in others
in a haste to empty their bowl

poetry also teaches compassion
if poetry succeeds, cats gather
around you at night
the warmth of the furry neck

3 29 04

prayer

brown slippers
blue & white striped cotton robe
dark brown-rimmed reading glasses

with acknowledgment
of my participation
in hurtful deeds

theft, cruelty, threat
uncaring, hurriedness

a seeking of wisdom
a finding humility

vanity, pride, idleness, sloth
mind like a mountain goat
jumping from rock to rock
trying to find a foothold

to hold strength in place

to be sad upon leaving
to form prayer hands
in dark sacred light
to be anonymous in an urban place
to find comfort in the discomfort

to hold in the heart a light
light & listening

3 29 04

western nebraska

the high school students from a
small town in nebraska, who were in
a 1947 ford, were surrounded by
cop cars in denver
the car had been mistakedly identified
as one seen leaving the scene of a crime
the three young men were questioned
& allowed to go on their way

breaking & entering, theft, destroying
government property, vandalism, throwing
rocks, snowballs, eggs at guards
stealing gas, fighting, playing war,
ditching school, drinking beer

hitchhiking 12 miles to sidney from
sioux ordnance depot
2 miles down a long hill, past an old
sod house, up over the viaduct, around
a curve, 10 miles east on highway 30,
the lincoln highway, past grain ele-
vators, past the red brick, 2-story,
schoolhouse, brownson, where whitman's
poems were memorized & dickinson's poetry
was taught
where soccer was played in the school yard
not far from train tracks
not far from fuckers' ledge
not far from the brownson tavern
not far from the baseball field
where bunker hill had its home games

my dad worked as a property supply
manager on sioux ordnance depot
s.o.d. employed 2,000 workers
it was an army supply depot: trucks,
jeeps, bombs …
the bombs were housed in igloos &
turkey huts & regularly the bombs

were destroyed
windows shook 20 miles from the explosions

we lived in a housing project: ordville
& we were surrounded by wheat on 3
sides & the depot to the east

school, sports, youthful love, mischief,
movies
i played baseball & basketball
i studied hard & got good grades
we hiked into the hills

we lived in a 2-bedroom apartment
in a long, rectangular, cinder block
building, which contained 4 units

i waited for a dark green army bus
to take me to grade school at brown-
son, to jr. high & high school in sidney
chimney town, we called ordville

4 13 04

to catch his breath

i met victor argo 40 years ago
in frank corsaro's acting class
victor was puerto rican
he was a strong & real
he was close with harvey keitel
they lived together for a while

in 1966, i began writing poetry
& by the end of the year, i had
a book ready to be published

victor was working as a printer
he stole 10,000 sheets of paper
(a heavier stock for the front
& back covers)
emma, who also studied with frank,
had a printing shop, allowed victor
to run off 300 copies
of my first book, *amarillo born*

one whole saturday, victor worked
the press, emma, rita, my girlfriend,
victor & i collated, max jeremy,
an artist, had contributed art
lee hickman had typed the poems
on a certain type of paper
& i had my first poetry book published
free

at that time, victor was also a fine
country singer
victor had been a club boxer in the bronx
he had been a refrigerator repair man

on saturday nights, i would meet vic,
harvey & robert haynie
at jimmy rae's on eighth ave. & 47th st.
& we would talk theatre

victor & i acted in "bus stop" at
the 14th st. theatre
i played bo, he was bo's sidekick

he had a great imagination
& he was always helpful to fellow actors
when we were both getting ready
to act in scorsese's "mean streets"
i talked to him about my role & scene
& what i wanted to create
that wasn't in the script & he encouraged me

we were also both in "boxcar bertha"
& "taxi driver" & he was saint peter
in "the last temptation of christ"

the last apartment my first wife, rita, &
i lived in was on columbus ave., between
77th & 78th streets — a 1-bedroom in
a bldg, with an elevator — we had a bed,
dresser, round wooden table, 2 straight-
back chairs, a rocking chair — rent
was $72 a month in 1968
we sold the apartment (rent-controlled)
& contents to victor for $300 & moved to l.a.

i miss victor very much
he also lived in l.a. for many years
& then moved back to his beloved n.y.c.
he would come to l.a. to work
or with harvey, & he would call me
& we would meet at farmers market
or at a restaurant on sunset &
eat a meal

he once told me that if it wasn't
for harvey, he'd be homeless

victor called me in late october of 2003
& told me that he was doing his first
broadway play
"anna & the tropics" opened on nov. 16th
& i saw him in a matinee performance
the following saturday
afterward, autograph seekers

called him santiago
he signed their programs

he called me in the middle of march
& told me that one of his lungs had been
removed & the cancer was gone
said he could only walk a block or two
before he had to stop for a while
"but it's better than the alternative," he said

a gracious man, a good friend, a splendid
actor

4 18 04

red snow fence

nebraska, where i threw baseball after
baseball against the cinder block
building: px, post office, barber shop
nebraska, where winds whipped snow into
white loaves against red snow fences
hypnotized drivers with ruddy faces
looking to get around the curve
& over the viaduct & up the long hill

from the southern central
to the furthest western state line of
two states
past point of rocks
a celebration of fort sidney days

baseball, hunting, first love, first
twisted, drunken, lostness with forever
troubling abstracted fear

to practice basketball, to race dad's car
past state line, to drink 3.2 beer at
joe's tavern at age 16
to drink from a keg of beer by a large
circular water tank with fellow class-
mates to vomit
to drink gin & orange juice in a white
chevy convertible, to take the french
exchange student to the christmas
cotillion, to puke on the lawn in front
of the high school, to break the window
in the front door with my fist, reach in
& open the door, fall drunk on the living
room floor
"harry, were you drinking last night?"

"wake up, little susie, wake up,
the movie wasn't so hot,
it didn't have much of a plot
wake up, little susie, wake up ..."
playing on the radio as i went to

the gym to help clean up the next
day after the dance
i had to apologize to the entire
senior class
i got kicked out of being president
of the honor society, of being lt.
governor …
all because genevieve abougie
said she wasn't going to let me kiss
her
when i decided to join the navy
to prove my manhood
when i made errors that summer
in baseball
when i realized i wouldn't make the
majors
when i realized i didn't have money
for college

my parents wouldn't sign, i was 17
& i finished high school
joined (july 7, 1958) the navy
my oldest brother & his wife were
at the swearing in, in denver

nebraska, where dirt roads, farms, small
towns, boyhood friends, libraries, base-
ball diamonds, wheat fields, hide-outs,
fences, bikes, theft, snow, hot summers,
pepsis & peanuts, fried chicken, roast
beef, sunday mid-day dinners, flags,
log cabin, silver dollar, brownson
tavern, brandin' iron, the mill, the
stag tavern, ksid, greenlee's, pip's
liquor, dalton's men store, boyd's cigar
store beckon me home
10th & illinois, 833 13th ave., 701 maple,
sioux ordnance depot, ordville, men's soft-
ball, bunker hill town team, sidney
firemen, sheriff schultz, carol swift
teaching "macbeth," carl crouse telling
us to write our speeches, "clear, concise
& to the point"
where i wrote 3 "i speak for democracy"
speeches & won all 3 high school

contests, 10th-12th grades
where i played basketball in the snow
outside on a dirt court
where i played basketball & baseball
first team for s.h.s.
where i won & lost & dreamed of playing
in the major leagues
where i loved pretty small town girls

4 20 04

quiet & forgiveness

it was 92 degrees today
& it's going to be 92 tomorrow
& it's still april

shorts & short sleeve shirt
& bare feet weather
cat on floor
in front of square fan weather
windows wide open
no quilt at night

one man talked of suicide
one talked against war
we eulogized a dead friend
one waved in the night

the man people blamed
became a winner

for often i find myself alone
with 4 cats
& some times they are like a circus act

the big bushy one rolls on his back
in front of the fan

the smell of gas was every where
& a helicopter began circling above
the older female chases the
younger female
who disguises poems disguises birth

4 26 04

memory

wooden floor
brown couch
black chest with gray cat sleeping
on top
square floor fan, round fan
rocking chair with tan cover
& 3 pillows
hat rack with worn white panama
& dodger cap
blue down jacket
white scarf black scarf
brown wooden filing cabinet
brown chair
rocking chair with green cover
with pillow & furry cat sleeping
love seat with white & gray cat
asleep
3 beige pillows
small wooden table
bookcase
2 paintings on wall above couch
3 photographs of step-granddaughters
record player on black table
cd player
2 speakers
clock vases pots photos
prairie of the urban heart

5 1 04

fabric torn

clouds of sheer tents
square light off shore
humiliation confused with violence

two friends spoke of death
one played his harmonica
threw it onto the casket

the other sat in the 10th row
was proud of his closeness
remembered things said

as if we were in a revolving
set of chairs
a yellow square light off right

bundles of light sparked
by memory by throwing by shooting
to set the river afire

life went out like lava
overflowing its path above black rocks
death sprung up
like yellow daffodils

happy shelling & streaks departing
behind blue heaven a female face
sensual cheek & hair & eye
moon & reflecting orange white sun
lake pale blue underneath

5 11 04

Everyday Things

jarmusch at the academy

holly & i ate at chef ming's,
crescent heights & santa monica blvd,
she had a glass of white wine
& i drank a bud light
we ate egg rolls, chicken with
broccoli & shrimp with lobster sauce

at 7, we left for the academy
gene was sitting down left, on the aisle,
& we sat behind him, & we talked
about his back, the memorial for
hubert selby, jr., dylan, the lakers

we saw "coffee & cigarettes," by
jim jarmusch, an enlivening film
made up of shorts shot over 18 years
with bill murray, rza & gza (wu
tang clan), iggy pop, alfred molina …
beautiful black & white

beckett-like, in its absorbtion to
smallness, routine, ritual, a reminder
of life's brief eternity
film is faces, & music of many moods
some people walked out
his films are not main-stream

in the car, on the way home, i spoke
of movies & theatres we went to — with
couples, friends, we knew
in bed, holly kissed me, "i love going
to the movies with you"

5 23 04

friendship

is give & take
each person holds
the other in his lap
like a cat
each heart opens
the drapes & looks
out
into darkness
each harm sleeps
each person listens
friends actually
are thankful
friendship goes
beyond gender
when one does
something for
the other the other
is grateful
a friend cares
has sympathy for
has happiness for

hardness falls away
friendship is jacaranda
tree blooming
is light in dark

5 25 04

friends

my eyes get tired these days
i arrange a poetry reading for diane
wakoski, who comes to l.a., with her
husband, robert turney, once a year

fred dewey, beyond baroque's director,
asks diane & laurel ann bogen to read
fred is one of beyond baroque's top four
people, along with george drury smith,
jim krusoe & sandy garrett

we have diane & robert over for dinner
the night before the reading
i compliment their shoes — his almost
red, her's brown
they look healthy
they tell us about the bukowski document-
ary they've seen that afternoon
at the nuart
after eating duck breast, corn pudding
& asparagus, i take them for a 2½ block
walk to de longpre, west of normandie
show them where i think bukowski
used to live

diane loves movies & we talk about them
i tell diane & robert that i am a member
of the student academy awards executive
committee at the academy & that about 30
of us, from different branches, watched 39
films, under 60 minutes each, from
countries around the world, & chose 5
for the entire body to view & vote
on — i told them about the student
documentaries
i voted for the one about young
cheerleaders, made by a berkeley
student
"they're like acrobats," diane said

i asked diane to sign her *discrepancies*
& apparitions, published by doubleday
in 1966, a hardback book i bought
in 1966, the year i began writing
poetry
"you matured early," i said
"i always believed in my poetry,"
she said

we ate chocolate cake with cream
cheese i had bought at the rose cafe
holly & diane showed each other
t'ai chi moves
they also talked about goddesses
they connected on those 2 subjects
they disagreed about hubert selby,
jr.'s "requiem ..."

we looked at robert's photographs:
nature, city, rooftops, specific
abstract, humanity, b&w & brilliant,
"you have quite a range"
grain elevator in nebraska
homeless man in new york city

she's a masterful poet
we enjoy their company
direct & honest & smart
well-dressed & homey, down to earth
yet learned

i value you
i value you like jacaranda blooms
i value you like movie houses
"to think you've had this book
all these years"

"i got nervous before you got here
& it wasn't anxiety about time"

6 1 04

a bowing

to honor
what has been
written
in the heart

a wife's love
a friend calling
me by my name

a cat waiting,
outside my door,
to be brushed

3 fellow poets
honor & cooperation

actors working
together, listening

a family with
memories of a
loving mother
a hard working
father

to honor my brother
who holds closeness
fast & compassion
faster

6 9 04

journey / stillness

in four days i fly to newark
where i will meet my sister, dorothy,
her husband, jim, my brother, jim,
& his wife, mae, at hertz rental
we will drive to a hotel & then,
on sat., july 3rd, & july 4th, we
will celebrate with bob & shio, & his
family, bob & shio's 50th wedding
anniversary

last sat. night, holly & i participated
in a poetry reading at beyond baroque
to herald a new publication: *beyond
baroque* mag.
the founder, george drury smith, was
there & i read my poem "honoring
beyond baroque's founder" to close
the reading
george came up to me afterward,
shook my hand, & was very warm to me
holly read two poems: a deep, clear,
resonant sound
the ex-coach of the lakers, phil
jackson, was there
i talked to him three times, gave
him a copy of *reunions*
"i've enjoyed your work; here's some
of my work"
for the most part, the night was
harmonious
5,000 copies of the mag. were printed

my brother, jim, said he & dorothy
are paying for my plane fare & hotel

tomorrow morning i am driving to ventura
to get a haircut from my friend, jack,
& borrow a suitcase
wed., i'll do the laundry
wed. night, holly & i are going to see

the dodgers play the giants
thur., i'll pack & withdraw $200 from
the bank
holly gave me a card with $100

rose has been staying close to me today
& tonight
holly thinks something is wrong with
her right eye & is going to take her
to the vet

family reunion, a celebration of marriage,
poetry, home
there is a shining light in my wife's
heart
that i see in the dark

my heart has a stillness tonight
while cars drive by on mariposa & fountain
sovereignty, a hope

6 29 04

newark airport

had a great time
celebrating bob & shio's
50th wedding anniversary

jim, mae, dorothy, jim & i
stayed at the marriott courtyard
we traveled together, ate together,
played hearts many times — mae won

we had a great dinner sat. night,
july 3rd, at rich & marie's
also present: chris & amy & their
children: kelsey & amanda;
robin, with her children: andre
& emily;
george & catherine

we shared family stories,
jokes, talked about work, sports
we signed a scroll
dedicated to bob & shio
andre & kelsey danced

it's rare & fun to be with our family
they have all done well

dorothy gave me "the deathbed
edition" of *leaves of grass*
newark to minneapolis / st. paul
to lax
holly kept the cats in
on the fourth of july

we went to a double-a
baseball game on the fourth
i sat by jim & mae, dorothy
& jim, george, shio & bob
a phillies' farm club vs.
an astros' farm club
beautiful stadium
a nuclear power plant in the distance

fireworks after the game
the last 2 songs were
"america, the beautiful," sung
by ray charles & "born in the u.s.a."
by bruce springsteen

i gave shio a hug
"say hi to holly," she said

7 5 04

he "slowed down time"

the movies give me solace
i watched "on the waterfront" again
with my wife, a week after brando died
valor & victory, vulnerability, heroic,
human tenderness, whitmanic — brando
he lives in our deeds — as we follow
brando, dean, cliff, voight, hoffman,
pacino, de niro
the heart has always got to be the master
so many of us fall to the money measure
seeking camaraderie amongst materialism
what of the human heart & what of
transformation

i loved brando in "... waterfront," "streetcar ...,"
"the godfather," & in "sayonara," "the young
lions," "burn," "last tango ...," "the chase"
he blotted out the sun
he brought us into the heart & anguish
of the man who named names & expiated
guilt
he was beautiful & bruised as a young man
he brought realism to "julius caesar"

he played bongos, he stood up for the black
panthers, the american indian, the van-
quished, the existentially lost
born in omaha, a rebel, a christ figure
being whipped in "one-eyed jacks," the
mythic framed western figure

he was a beautiful figure on the screen

7 11 04

rare garden

god is a collective thing
it is never more than the individual

suffering never changes anything
it goes hand in hand with compassion

one cat sleeps near four
two males, two females, two young, two
older

my family has many ages
my father died in 1967
my mother died in 1970

my oldest brother is 82
my second oldest brother is 80
my sister is 78
my brother closest to me is 66
in two months i will be 64
my wife is 66
my son is 35

my brother closest to me & his wife
& my sister & her husband & i ate
sausages, potatoes, scrambled eggs,
blueberry pancakes, waffles, cereal,
toast, we played hearts in the court-
yard, the airport, we laughed

god is a challenge i never give up

7 11 04

the work

there was a shaft of light
on my manuscripts at 3:51 a.m.

in my mind, in sleep, i had been
thinking about principal roles

i had played in films, tv, commercials
the thought & sum of preparation

what exists what had not existed
i received the script of "the silence

of the lambs" 2½ months before
i began shooting & i borrowed a pigeon

named champ, kept him in a cat cage
outside on the patio, brought him in

for an hour a day, learned how to hold
him, spent time with him in the bedroom

with newspapers spread throughout
talked to him, fed him, we became mates

he liked to fly & land up high
on the windows' curtain rods

i chose my costume, one of layers for
a man who worked outdoors in the cold

in cincinnati, wore a knit cap
with the colors red, gray & blue

hammered nails daily, toughened
my hands, practiced my lines

created a visual for the opening
of the first exterior when clarice

starling walks up to me, "mr. bimmel?"
i would be holding a white

racing pigeon up to the sun, opening
a wing, looking for mites

jonathan demme, the director, asked
me before, "what do you want to do

in this scene?" i told him, he said
"great" & shot it

the production designer called me
a month & a half before my scenes

were to be shot & asked for personal
photos to use in the upstairs' bedroom

scene & i sent photos of baby dylan
& me & they were framed & used

as well as others that the film's
photographer took of mr. bimmel & his

daughter "who went for a job inter-
view in chicago & never came back"

7 18 04

comic books

the thorpe family was a tall family
robert was my age & anna
a few years older
they could have been a basketball team

when i was 11, i used to take a stack
of comic books over to their home
& trade comics with the whole family

i would sit on the sofa & mrs. thorpe
would give me a stack of comics
to look through
she would also give me a coffee can
full of sunflower seeds to eat

one night, i tapped on anna's window
& she lifted up the window
& she let me feel her breasts

i always used to think it was funny
that grown-ups read comic books
& that i traded comics with a whole family

7 24 04

l.a. premiere of "the manchurian candidate"

holly & i had good seats, reserved,
down left, half way in from the aisle
we sat next to allison anders, who
directed "gas, food, lodging" & "mi vida
loca"

the movie was brilliant, provocative &
powerful
demme covered me with two good shots
i am always grateful to be in his
movies

afterward, i ate a small roast beef
sandwich, chicken on a skewer,
a shrimp, mashed potatoes with cheese,
salad, pasta, & 2 small chocolate
cakes & a decaf

holly & i talked to roger & julie
corman — they are a delight

before the movie started, holly
& i sat & talked with john aprea
& his daughter, nicole
john also acted in the movie

i saw charles napier & tracey
walter — they were in the film
& have been in many demme films

i gave demme a hug
& praised the movie, "stunning"
he said, "you did magic"

julie corman said, "harry, you
always bring something extra
to your roles"
she was born in omaha

julie talked to holly about
prose poetry

demme hired me 3 times in the
seventies
3 times in the eighties
3 times in the nineties
once in 2003

7 27 04

Recluse

4-12-05 to 9-27-05

Recluse

the worm

there was a long worm
about the size of a telephone pole
in width & depth
& a block long in length
its face was like the top of a
telephone pole
only rounded & friendly
with eyes & a mouth

it traveled on the ground
beside me
it was smooth & flexible
we traveled past a car wash
past a taco truck
past people working, people eating

the people looked at the worm
the worm looked at me
& i smiled, "it's okay"
we continued on our way

4 12 05

beyond

the door never ends
even though stones on the left
to dry
the spirit was called
to come home
to come down

a door lifted
pushed aside
a stone put under
to keep the door open

the door must be a breath
an adversary to forsake
to go back would be afraid

not when called
later
of its own will
the door, sorrow
of its own, without

5 16 05

congregate in dark

a face made of a thatched basket
interlaced with modesty, honesty
& a golden light inside

one eye like the earth with
a red eyebrow patch

flowers, 3 yellow mums, spring
from an ear

a steel bar, wheel
strike the heel
heart has always had a turning

the face must
have alleys & matches
a place to walk alone
made of vanity & ambition
wings like a scythe
lighted jukebox at the table
whisper hearts must die
it turns & walks by an apple
big as a tree with a leaf atop

the three sunflowers

cool evening fall
has its eyes far above schism
constant diagonal crossings:
swords, path & light

light above from below
chapel, mountain, corridors
thatched cabins, with reins,
in early sunlight
zebras of corn, shafts
fallen like a key extinguished

his feet, fleet, flourishes of light,
fire forever from wounds

6 2 05

morning: repetitious movement

hands up, a perimeter glow
piano keys & arm of a sofa
from the puffed sleeves
fire about to lighten

a man sleeps before the city
he sees a woman in her bed
purple covers tucked round
fog, tripod, soldier of old

blood spilled before the fallen
her legs, lovely, lid, fire
about to be lifted
indigo wrist band, twisted hair

pulled, movement through snow
gold, gloves, a flipping
light off the armor
one arm bare, red, crooked

she sits forward, shoulders bare
brushes tree, over snow
light under door, as she reclines
her face filtered by light abrupt

she sleeps in shadow
lake & daybreak, edges of
worn threads, tied & throat
back, table, cloth, wheels

red, auburn as the hills
her breath lifted, protected
thrust, kiss, downpour
each morning glistens, red bow

a curtain opened, azure blue
blood tumbles, bracelets, circles
of light above the darkened
perimeter of a lady's face

6 2 05

take my heart & multiply

what is the soul
if it isn't a yearning
for the truth?
it is breath

door, ache, heart
the jet rises above daffodils
a going outward soul
unrolls, falls
walks among threats

death, fire, landslide
money, celebrity, fame
soul celebrates curving swords
shacks with hands:
oranges fall

tonight, i talked with an old friend
about film, documentaries, youth
where is the soul
if not in communion?
it's in death
& honoring the passing of a poet

each time i'm with poets
i love, it's like i'm in a church
on my knees giving thanks
among the feet of white cows

a simple water wheel
water also has soul
in the ringing of bells
ears of corn, grapes, friends

the word made from mind &
heart, rhythm, a person
darkness precedes us
it tears up the holes in our
anguished monologues
where i doubt, i begin

who never had a memory of his father
the dark horses & fire behind

6 4 05

ocean-like flame trails

a fan as big as a ship
big as a butterfly
gray
a yellow wing with tinges
of gray & white
turns into a lady's bracelet

shining light
like the flame
of a cigarette lighter

black rock crashing
into the water's flame
finally, a moving boat
under the spider web

hand, stairs, deer
street lamp
a blue-beige shade
rings like a bell
wheels, snow, path
all golden barbed wire circles

skis down, sleds over
rowers, speeding from oncoming

the icy blue waters
submerged by a golden harvest
it rushes across the continent
forever the ark, tossed
a cross, threshhold, lights below,
above

a man in a boat, rows
there has been a shaft of light
from above, & around
with hands, above regal blue cloth

white irises tall as skyscrapers
spider webs like butterflies
burst

furrows & circles of fire roaring
mask, face, belt, body
sword that stretches into the sky
like a lonely ship crashes
waterfall & fire & large turning wheel
like a fan like a water of fire
the train's smoke blurs into sunset
white ash barren tree
her dress a flame with silver sash
she sleeps on high, a space open

6 4 05

reaching up to hold

in hollywood a pen slanted
a twister, tumbleweed, a
six-shooter the figure 4
lawn of ladies rare, devotion

mountain, the pen up against rain
like spears each sign of A
devotion spurs across the sky
young athletic boys delivered books

fire in the far dark
rare because it was more than
opportunity seized
fire was near like a state

a foreground love
stunned, swept, yellow panes
above the door frame, rhapsody
baskets of pink peonies

yellow flowers keep returning
fence yellow & there was friendship
feathers in hair turned into hills
of red roses

circling a giving devotion to a
bursting flower with lightning
strikes aslant
half circles round like sun energy

scarlet clouds surround
moon-tossed green leaves
feet baby blue
mint green tinged narrow stems

red flowers shoot up like bees
boat of white flowers & waves of
red, & road downhill, white turns
golden, human fall

pen, blue-green, down into boat
like a dagger, pens the boat's sides
parallel with dark waters with
light splashing

pen cuts like scissors & rocks
lights across the cradle's bow
dives into green water to retrieve
sunset reflected, again, calm, boat

5 6 05

a sole shaft of light

the letters were red
written on blue
& the letters
looked like barbed wire
& danced a tune
& walked, musical notes

square window
rain dropped an explosion
silver burst
red spelled out
walked through mint green
upstairs, spread wings
like a bat

water was everywhere
& troubling
down earth's curve
& splashed up silver-white
a yellow-green butterfly
roses unfolding, unfurling

like golden trumpets outward
3 orange geraniums
a whole windowsill full

for the eyes turn
like grapes like ants
wings mint green
above white roses

white wings tinged pink
guardians
slashes clouds smoke
explosions atop
above the soldiers

calm down & face upturned
hilltop savior
twisting figure
band of red, black band

skull, flight path to top
of hill
wings are spread up & down
rifles slanted toward sky
along the ramparts, fired
& all the black figures fall back
wings are the perimeter
a cliff around the fallen
white figure along abstract
horse & rider uphill & fall back

6 9 05

light into the animal head

remembers out through the circular
echo amidst lightning strikings
until calm
above a pond

awning a wide curtain above
an axis, mask darkness cuts into
her legs slightly bent
in lavender, fence white

body forward
wind at turn
a funnel up through
finally a room with chair, quiet

room by room she goes
until she finds her
shafts of wheat held downward
her face to the side of a shining

depth among many squares
openings
flower next to woman reading a book
blue & gold grace

a chest inlaid with golden moons
pale scarlet extends, falls shadow
her wrist & arm revealed
leans & nods & moves forward

striped wallpaper, white & green
face, triangle, swiftly withdrawn
small bell held by a hand
brushed

curtain brushes blinds
she opens one door, closes it, opens
another door amidst flashes of light
bed white & lush

sword unsheathed by bedside
white bells like daffodils upturned
swinging on line in a breeze
held & lost an open darkness

her nakedness lifted & turned
fresh light, trees, lights wave
flooded light in the kitchen window
a shade once more the darkness

6 10 05

hurries to catch

the road emerged
from the mouth
her feet white, hunt
she looks under, waits

diagonal tracks
where he & 3 friends
played a pickup baseball
game called "automatic"

the white path down
her chest, a center
of gold rushing
surrounded by round stones

he heard "blackhawk,
dave brubeck, franchot tone"
"not one senator voted
against the war"

he saw her reach under
the woman sits half-naked,
she rises, waves, two doors
open & close

light around an orb
"reagan, residuals" older
actors read a play written
by an older writer, free meal

he sees a light afar
like a drive-in movie
seen from the highway
light dances like indians

around fire, he seeks
camaraderie, quiet, he sits
calmly, listens
the dark train merges

boyhood, retirees, animal,
shifting light — she walks
away, turns, comes back
looks under — lights like

elk horns dancing, fiery,
rolling hot sun, rose
where the hit ball bridges
light underneath spider crawl

6 11 05

Summer Solstice Healing

summer solstice healing

a long tunnel with yellow sparks,
fiery, arrows of light shone forth
to the right & down, the tail burst
apart, blood cross, mask, eyes light

screen like a net, crab-like form,
one eye, antennas whirling, a long
worm with many feet — candles
& berries — eye & eye looking up

mint green arms & the creature swims
turning breeze, golden bells above
the pools of light diagonally elevate
earth moves away, red figures jump

away like sunbursts, a golden sun-
flower about the forward face moving
toward angel light, forlorned figure
climbs aboard, roaring light above

the castle, circular light in blue
revolutions — fire, fires like roads
a man arises from sleep, rolls over
like waterfalls, divine, memory

a lighthouse in the field's center
love, hope, sorrow, light like fire
descends the hill, racing
quiet upsweep, a turtle-like armor

in the heated blast — arrows jet up
rockets strike down & out
for all the upsweeps water
an eye surrounded by mint green

sees, moves centers, opens full rays
above the upturned city & trees
growing downward, blood red ripeness
turn, surely turn, cool, a magenta

burst-love, with wings, white horse
hand forward, into dark red, with
bull & rings, silver, encircled
our feet in blood, rails of blood

white wings, black body, green eyes
golden chair in sky, in motion,
hands & body out of flower, relent-
lessly bright, half apple, half moon

6 21 05

diagonal upsweep

somehow, it's like looking at the
red rock, a side of mountain with light
striking it
the long & narrow waterfall with
a house next to its southern side
a hand with white perimeter points
down as rockets shoot up & a beak
lifts
rocky foreground, monument valley
in the background
raven turns blue, white like
shafts of wheat, moves into air
large birds against the strikes
a roll of waves their bodies

golden horn, trails of dust
we hide under dark wings at dusk
golden arrows break through bone
burning wrists, triangles of sails

men swim in the air, circular up-
sweeps, tunnels of emerging
wings split, rush round azure polar
caps, a single half moon

what reason, what insists, what point-
ed corners, full light in corn, blood
before onrushing center golden light
with surrounding orbs around face

like a windshield, a rear view mirror,
sweeps back & forth, shines down
over fields, river through autumn trees
black ants surround an open, gold box

black grapes, bees full, peaceful sky
blue with clouds, pastoral
low clouds above rectangular houses
where on earth the light goes up

yellow brandishing light!
wings bright, sparkling as smashing
windshields, opens wings full — body
straight & central as city hall
candle straight & high horizon burning
with sword & mane like vatican
bright in wavy skyline
my home my heart my single light
in dark, steps down covered in white

6 24 05

trees & an arrow

star explodes like hatchet thrown
horn turns ensemble red & blue
alley with trees' shadows
curving sword cuts lock
darts, circles, tremendous propulsion
bright & clean sidewalk after rain

processional, opens, comes up aslant
seats on a train, magenta sky
circular movement, lotus blossoms
just that one pink flower in lake

rain, train moves through leaves
no more orchards, circles, lines, rods
through tunnel, steps upward
purple grapes like bees' hives

arrows blood-tipped, pointed downward
like all the deaths about to come
surrounded, life brief diamonds, horses
rich, red roses, for wilderness gone

blue, red-tipped, flowers, our arms
reaching past fields of corn, golden
harvests, sunset, train curves, smoke

rockets shoot through the sky
sunburst, spools of white through
names, destinies, gold exhaust jettings

like single armbands, single golden
arrow
when it stops, the heart breaks in
ignorance

bright flower bursts upward
simple light, door, descending steps
cleaning, sleeping, waking, present light

greenness surrounds lake, lake surface
turns blood-like

each train with empty seats, each
blooming flower

flower bloom upward like rockets
exploding, & circles red leaves
like horse & rider, like ship with sail
many horses & fighting, wheat brushed
back against the train-smoked sky
indians leaving, one tree, red leaves
bodies, tumbleweeds, rust, golden vase

6 30 05

in the night the light has always been shining

a face that has the 4 corners in it
face in light like coin like roman
with open hand
moving past roads
face against face to make one
for the green paths through lavender
like birds & a faraway song
beehive honor hourglass
face on coin face on stamp
lights like lemons under ladders
fires gushing shoulders
an opening to a tent, a path

rusted car in field
silver eye, sash & the beak over
like a night cap

windmill covered wagon journey
half circle, riders
shining eye
white wings spread

light comes down from 2 angles
broken light cuts cross blue-grayness
for shadow in the abstract red luscious
cross
golden & red alternating stripes
to speak under
a bridge a meteor

place to rest place with shadows
criss-crossed rothko face
propped & receded
roads & stripes across it
darkness up & lightness down

single flame, candle bright, springs
like arms opened, upward, silver
badge shaped light with musical notes
dancing, floating out & above
sky above arm below

row of scarlet row of gold
above eye — sheds, gushes gold again
distinguishes light between two
darknesses

7 17 05

to determine

the age, bright & octagonal, like
a swimming pool, central, exting-
uishes itself

somber sunset
a man shot by police snipers,
who had been watching the building
he emerged from
he was told to stop & he ran

the age black on black slide
with few stars in the night above
the tv screen

from pakistan — tombstones
golden leaves like alms
around a darkened tunnel a light
curves

four men on different screens
each man wears a backpack

face, made of rain on golden apple,
emerges
sunflowers afire

the golden arrow, revolving, spans
west to east
a white rose spinning upward
to be named would be to kill its end-
ing

fire at its foot & sweeps runway
a boat away — smoke
single white spire, asymmetrical shoe

held in his arms, golden tablet, tv
screen
the river rushes toward its fall
a fire in its middle
& the curving entrance has a fire

the age, red & hot as a revival, forced
in on itself
branches, street light
the city, intermittent water, last seen
on a map
the curved light downward like a
sword
animal runs after footsteps

7 26 05

sheets of alphabet like rain

the J equals
JJ like shoes walking
artillery guns shooting
knife 1 way
explosions the other
burning foot raised upward

an oval bright light
moves diagonally
an eye then a face
twisting spinnings

feathers curl down around
to include a rocking runner
oval light jumps to touch
lit finger & hand golden

darkness appears with green
perimeter — armor golden
lake at blue-gray time
sheds forth water wheel
colors tears denote time
cut through petals
up under the ceiling

lighter face till light
narrows until only the eye
has a home under black sails

long cylindrical light shoots
horizon — rolls back & lifts hand
bright room winding unto
city bridge canal water
golden wings above door

movies cannot save me in the soul
exposure

8 14 05

detachment to be my youth

silver with a light at top
road around
kneeling, light jets to right horizon
wings of light

key guitar smashed
fuel light under turning propeller
in the center a quiet light

what was youth if not desire
thought exterior image interior
told, now must die

alphabets like rain above summer
clouds dark rolling
face upward
curls thunders bursts
sunlight deep mine spotlight

who can deny alternating seasons
theft honor rain white bad heart
roundness shoulder worth profile
face hawk hurls twists beak

tornado with its dark light
turning quiet
hand upward propels horizon

shovel, red
wings gold, upraised
bright & holi
golden figure across sky

light diaganol
thunders down sky's mountain
like giant surf riders
or a field ready for morning

held & circled in darkness
animal scent, love cleans

golden figure rests atop mountain's
cathedral

swoops down, golden figure
into blue background, tambourines
sparkle, breath apple scroll
diagonal shafts of light protect tree
golden sashes remain

8 15 05

recluse of light

the path between two circles
has light & jewels in its eyes
begins to leave ripples
encircles in on itself
white flowers shaped like propellers

fresh wood — hermes in its head
for the lead light, like diamond
carried on the shoulders
past white house with green awnings
an arrow around

animal feet, white leaves
one door opens, the animal rushes
to meet, door closes, another
door opens & the eyes bleed gold
forever goes to meet

the path has many steps made of
emerald, golden light
eyes surrounded by darkness
lines, circles, curves — spring &
unfold — silver sparks & saxophone

seclusion, green valley & then a
rolling disc, giant wheels turn
golden wheat, grain elevator, moon
full & golden also, an eye above a
dark ship, pushing in the darkness

our land, eagle feathers, proud
light above a hand above
bow untied — a loom & then the blue steps
reflection of light ahead
wide prairie, deepening canyon, sunset

hand & face, side to ground
with circles of nests (locusts, wasps,
wings spreading) carry golden in blue
through the emperors of twilight
blots out half the light, swirls upon

& then the red blood bow sash across
horizon, golden coffin shapes
from out of the earth, a long
narrow ladder, opened ovals of light
owls, wings spread, folds upon folds
light shines down, pale white petals

8 19 05

an offering

the window
dispatches rubbing shaking
full light then blue river
a car a shape of light like texas

light like book or wrist watch
it came to greet with love
each morning outside the door
for the rustling tumbleweeds ahead

returns, a beak out of the light love
each regular morning, cleans
but the darkness with only a face
has a white rose at center, emerges

siren & two lights, bridge, shore
with arms reaching toward narrow
boats — wood through the window
racing up the coast — golden explosions

lines & circles & islands, hope, love,
a bridge of light — the dwelling
must not shed darkness — cuffs of
light to grab & hold to deny hidden

unwrapping of the linen-clad face
one eye, religious even, folds of white
about the neck, red turban, alligator-
shaped scepter — golden head above

the crowd, bejeweled, with side shafts
of light — beginning propeller turns
& makes shadows, cleans heart, repose
a warmth in bed — egypt, assyria,

sumer — hall of many golden icons
raining — long gray path & a
bell-shaped sweeping tone — jagged
silver ceiling, dark body, white face

cathedral, light at front, rise to be
broken & stretched in a picasso painting
turned into blood-dark chorus, golden
fabric around the heads — columns,

arches, arms, webs of bridges upward
in wealth brightness, the lovemaking
& red grapes — figure above figure
golden tree, leafless, pure gold in dark

8 21 05

Emerald Wings

our hearts

the blue path falls down
sprinkled with golden threads
liveliness, love, a pointing to
the mouth to be kissed, a circle

of gold & a patch of lavender
for our hands are always apart
& reaching toward each other
the long line of gold on the horizon

parallel to the youthful highway
circle of gold around the trees
a lone saxophone player on a swing
& the golden arrow cuts into blood

waiting with emerald hearts
a long golden worm curves
a ship in blood & sky thou has asked
strands of light above the head

& wagon, jagged half circle of light
mask, mouth, endurance, thankfulness
up on a cliff, royal blue nest
straight down fast furious light!

the patterns have met & gone home:
mask, triangle, arrow, rectangle,
like a train across the horizon, an
early ladder down — light, sky, earth

close to its axis, our hands turn
drill & cross & pummel & revolve
trees beside the long blue train
& knives thrust upward, surrounded

by thousands of trees — the rushing
leaves forward — solitude past
anguish — waves rushing up & returning
tree, plane, clearing

blue waters curl, fall, a golden path
resides in our hearts, circles above
the clouds — punches, thunders
hears a single man amidst all dead

feathers thrown from the sky
sunflower wheels, prairie, smoke
corn, scythe, revolving, path through
the corn — light strikes, golden path

8 24 05

harvest

bless you for this heart in your
hands
bless you for anguish, solitude,
camaraderie
bless you for intermittent light
bless you for the golden, diamond,
encrusted cross
bless for the breath of water,
the tongue of cat, the blue water-
falls
bless for the changing & healing
emotions
bless you for the locked door, the
closed door, the open door

bless you for brothers, sister, wife
& son
bless you for the long quiet path
bless you for the shadow of the
door

bless denial & acceptance, window
& seeking

bless the hand that holds words

bless nature with its eye
bless claw & tummy, turning & resting
bless lostness & the light about with
its birds
bless foot & eagle & crow
bless hiding place
night & hunt

bless holding high religious symbols,
apple & hat, heart & sadness & the
golden chariot with its smoke

bless outward & coming home
bless jeremiah, isaiah, micah & mark
twain

bless that one emerald faraway eye
bless terror & wings & fall
bless bed & wife, cat & door
bless amarillo & bless santa monica
bay
bless the mundane & the clusters of
sunflowers!
bless the vertical revolving sash & the
white cow of heaven

8 24 05

home

home, masks of light
spider webs lit up
indian face dissolves
lights shine throughout neighborhood

lavender dress with lights sparkling
car, hand, window
blue eyes like cars at a drive-in
with their lights on

perimeter of lightning strikes
twirling skirts, magenta chair
green arrows hit the shield
hand has light at its wrist

blood at forehead
light through the trees
hands come together to form
the skull of a cow

a figure in blue light dances
rubs the base of the animal's back
fire starts low, figure emerges
an eye, a steeple, circle & foot

mouth hand tail leaf
figure crucified — light straight
hair golden, on fire, green dress,
blue, wide waterfalls

body waits, like a figure in the sky
light like a road with turns, traveled
face, buddha, breaks into, retains
fullness, a quiet surrounding

mouth, wide as a canyon, golden teeth
multiple ships with sails on ocean
like a crown — one sails close
jets of water trail

barbed wire about the neck & face
hand with blood at center
twirling, crashing waters
blue bay, sensuous arm & leg

waterfalls higher, peaceful top
shades of golden & tan grains across
like a flag — propeller still
golden bed, dark blue sky, stars
the turning under, lavender skirt,
one rose, wide & red, sleeping face

8 26 05

burning above chalice

the lights are skyfull
twirling, spangling, a heart
beating inside the folding, sprawling
like bright belts coupling

a bison, a woman's head back
upon the red bed, her body
a perimeter of red
the pattern seems to be

one of twisting & rolling
a bush bright light, a spine
surrounded by gold in darkness
light above explosion & a thrusting

upwards — woman's face — indian's
face feathers (two) behind
moon blooms trumpets
white flower upward, leaves around

gardenias drape black & white cow
flower spins, cuts & jets
& tender red roses circle diagonally
her head & neck

single white flower, body
turns round
white in blue sky & the white
shoots outward

all directions aslant, up & down
the yellowness with carpet
unfolding downward
a figure sitting in golden chair

glass, circle, memory, vertigo
golden seven shaped like scythe
golden sails, ship, feminine face
force of light shot out like fire

wall, ancient face, part emerald
head top, the dark lines touch
in square, at center white
propeller like white petals

golden figure with wings in light
an open blue sky above green field
the figure's body the earth, half
light, half dark, a trumpet, a kiss

8 28 05

comes near for companionship

the road leads past skies
it's a bowl waiting for hands
lavender background
a golden cow & a hand down

there are roads around the wall
golden ringlets at the bottom
& perimeter of the bed
the road has a clock

she's half-naked in the heat
of the night
all can be eaten but the shell
what was once was

fire beyond the fence
a revolving whiteness in the middle
of golden wheat
houses, snow, at the foot of mountains

face of golden next to blood red
but the children by a fence, windy
again, golden arms circle
fingerprint, white eagle, royal blue

sunset, tall green trees with
white arrows pointed at tops, east
& west, & a face with a red path
coming out of the mouth

the rectangular window has a
golden curve inside the frame
scarlet & golden musical notes
at the base of a gigantic egg

the dark trees move forward,
like men on skis with rifles
the wings are light green & the
eyes flutter seductively

been here — golden path across the
football field — a golden cross
with scarlet perimeter, out of &
above the same colored bricks

light, like meteor, shoots toward,
seeks to join the sun, golden circle
around the milky way — an eye,
a bridge, two eyes with light forward

8 28 05

resounding, golden rings

a plane coming in at an angle
a circle of perimeter light
with a golden base
earlier, there was a silver sword

meteor of golden light curves
round & down
finally, parallels the many cars
at night with lights on

on circles of freeways, straight-
aways & cloverleafs
chair above, half in shadow, quiet,
regal

the connected, golden belt
breaks away, wings & silver spine
the depth is there without force
light, like a hand of cards,

opens up, fans out
green-winged figure flies
cross the dark sun
rays of light stream above the

golden crown — no war for a
woman's beauty — the piercing
green figure stretches in a doorway
hair down & shadows behind

mask, cathedral, face turns into
white rose unfolding — winged bug
transforms into an early plane
flying sideways at an angle

rose, eye, body, warm, breeze
constant unfolding petals
turning & moving cross time length-
wise — a far square gold, wraps

side of mountain, face, fish, white
luscious, richly folds of rose — comfort
an eye & her naked body, head turned
one way, right arm the other

green opening, boat comes through
refreshing, white upclimb
white rose dominates, outer petals
fold back revealing lavender, face
caresses & holds her in a golden staircase

8 30 05

emerald wings

on upraised sword, parallel with
another one
white rose — a hand picks a petal
from the center

sheds its petals as it turns
fire, night, explosions
burning in the background
white tiger

cow, gray sheep — lamb asleep
white waters fall to shore
a mouth for sleeping
cuts down, through big waves,

with wings — for the deaths have been
indecent — wheels move like turning
cinema — leaves, roses, folds furious
white — in the center turning each

way, quiet kitchen, white with
emeralds, a small boat being rowed
in a giant wave, whirls inward,
deep downward arrow through blue

can we hold our hearts
shafts of light slant downward
light pink roses in light
light green roses, shoulders & rows

winged horse climbs into dark sky
columned bridge, over water
white horse with rider moves toward
hands, fingers, tips upward like guns

broad expanse with one thick, rust-
colored tree — white-winged bird
circles cow with jewelled beetles
up its side in a swath

reclining elk in center of lit
baseball field — arrows against my
will — white birds, wing — still,
suddenly black paths curve upward

winged white bird with green apple
white rabbit moves cross horizon
elephant, beautiful wings with sun-
tinged circles of honeycomb

8 31 05

sunflower fire

her dress was full & had light
at the center, billowing colors
wings on the figure, hearse with
magenta flowers

winged figure skis, yellow petals
dark center, small winged figures
like snow flakes, revolving energy
golden horned bull, light splashing

like children running through water
spray from a hose, crescent moon
flowers tied to a horizontal wire
young boy on winged horse climbs

bow & arrow against onrushing stones
immense quietness before a tornado
women & children watching from their
front door steps — umbrellas, hats, fans

violets, warmth, near, purple around
white face moving, lightning, dark
greenness moves upward, golden harp
large as a door, white flowers from

the neck up, royal blue flowers
& a cracking white, the golden
cross will not let go — ship staggers,
with boat aboard, the ocean,

the man, the lostness, the relaxing
& upward sweep, fire behind many
rows — dagger, plant, plane, cutting
off at the base — pure white above

the shootings — wings coming from
above the eyes, scarlet & golden
rug unfolding, half shadow, half
golden circle — prepositions of swords

allegiances to fire & flowers
peacock bright, bouquet of scarlet
her face finally, golden, large as the
earth, sad, one piercing green eye

waterfalls, fence, serene up her
misty blueness, white around the tree
splashes of gold around the deep
blue water, thin gold mask, red lips
dark bruised center, blue cross, light

9 1 05

golden birds beside

the river ran straight down
& had a bowtie, had a crescent
had white gravestones beside it
at one point, white birds above

white flowers & jets
had a history of gunplay
a horn of plenty
people came walking

what was born was also destined
the green kept appearing
with a spotlight
it had yellow flowers on it

half circles along a side
sensual, still, circles above & steps upward
red with gold filaments
blue baseball caps

as they moved past the sheets drying
sweeping, pushing, beneath what holds
us — through the city, by a waterfall
white waters beside big timber

hand with boat
candle burning in boat on water
her silk dress
naked beside each other

legs & logs & cowboy boots
a golden face above the stringed bridge
like a harp, at daybreak, at sunset
carried us beyond our dreams

up the tall buildings, windows,
steps — the boat shoots the fast
rapids, its trail like a peacock
circle of green moves up the arm

missouri, mississippi, ohio, colorado,
platte, snake, columbia — a land
beyond the blue mist
a circle of light on the canyon wall

lines, circles, crescents, returns
white journey above the next hill
darkness, greenness on each side
her golden hair, white wings, glide

9 2 05

transparent wings with emerald

white handkerchief twirls into
a sombrero
lightnings crosses
white rose with small arrows

circling round
golden winged man on horse
golden hand reaches up & grabs
eye of orange & green

fire circles down a mountain
like a road
wheel, belt, wraps around
bed, white belt

tiger, bull, large winged insect
hercules helmeted
wolf with light strikings at right side
somber, still, fires around

a white house on its side
eye with white wings carrying it
telephone line with white birds
snow, train, bus — worship turning

large golden letters like graffiti
white-winged figure in scarlet
robe & golden crown — light sparkles
straight band of light — bands of

light like trains across the sky
a face back with tan bison
etched in the eye like an arrow,
pierced — horses across, leaves blown

round light shines down, round
light shoots blessing from forehead
escaped, alongside a mountain river
quiet within — golden star — giant

tree, waterfalls alongside
figure, its spine silver pieces
face with crown — bent legs
its eyes bulging silver, giant spider

light like a feather out one eye
its belly a roof of light like fringes
cut at its belly's center — waving
flowers like wings, golden legs

9 3 05

church door star

two hands palms down
narrow rocket plane straight up
white propeller
shadow moves across the screen

propeller like a dress
dances — shade up slightly
anchor aslant
woman's face

streaks of yellow light
green vertical field
with crumbled gold band
light churns half the globe

yellow arrow
giant tree like a butterfly
with road through it at base
yellow sky above dark field

with yellow tail
wings secure spread wide
her face rests — light brown hair
curls — warmth

dark eye lashes, orange square nose
cat sits under chair, rich fur
fox, alert face, giraffe, fire out
from height — cloud like yellow

flower — half circles float
moon slowly waxes on screen
at end of football field
golden wings spread down, touching

earth — the shooting light alongside
fox face — golden leaf under its chin
rests in love's shadow — hand like a
pharoah's scepter — wings with

rocket fire at body's base
candle flames in a row — her face
back, she turns, rests — the rich fur
white light out of the turning

light comes from all angles to a corner
golden cylinder with brown spots at top
face with darkened eyes, revolving light
golden figure in blue revolvings, dark
bands across the heaven, yellow bouquet

9 3 05

white figure, arms upraised

the white lights sparkle
wide white wings
& a hand upside down & open
fire moving through darkness

spreads its tail down
house top, white arrow, tree
bow tie, belt, white curving road
single square golden shaft opens

boat, in rough waters, near shore
triangle, coast, golden & red sashes
white horse lifts up neck near trees
bridge — sun behind

knives, with black handles, pointing
to center, river, boat, flames across
landscape with cross hairs
& the gold curves down a hill

shadows, tiger, cubs — all washing
themselves — big gray-tan lion
rises — fox in furrow — insect with
black eyes, white pupils, large wings

dam, golden field below
great cliffs — all the falling
pieces (gray metal) from plane
light, bone-shaped, in insect's mouth

a serpentine earth, green — anti-air-
craft guns shooting — white arrow
river, sky, wide river with bridge
arrow again — demanding yet demure

tree, branches with no leaves, streak
of light above, chairs & fire light
a horizontal figure in front of
the seated men — winged fire on left

& right — rushes & sand — the men's hats
are lit candles — they sit around a
table & there are fires in a city, in
doorways — a path of fire from a chapel

rolling white ocean waves — bird flies up
divided sky — light comes below — a white
tree, large white hand, trumpet, twirl-
ing cylindrical, figure, violets strewn
upward, white figure, white bird on shoulders

9 4 05

circle of flame on water

earth, the river has fallen,
golden wings — white blaze
man on horse, all white, arrows
stuck in his shield — light down

& ship in far background, half-circles
turn round — boat moves forward
thrown into space — arrows, upside
down, curved, in green — diamond

green like light of day beginning
bottle, chair in outline, man walks in
water, enters across — tree goes up
like a hand — leaves green & gold

curved, vertical lines on four sides
roof fallen with shoes under
black circle comes forward & explodes
hundreds of lines aslant in light

like nets in blue, like ships at near
shore's side —figure in center, wrapped
in white — box, ready to jump, heroic
like a burst of flowers, white & green

never have so many hearts twirled,
drilled diagonally like a diamond
& a white up rush with house, small,
on top, stationary, saxophone all

shiny in golden lines, roads circle
the music continuum like a tree
bursting upward into sunburst
building, floors, ships — flood — ships

flood the city once again, rolling
pipes, friction given off — saxophones
lines marching — golden horns upward,
outward — fires at end of

spears, in wagons, clearing, stakes,
leaves — quietness with large, green
tree, symbol, like a city, still, alone
then golden light hits the side of

buildings, an arrow up, a large
golden circle, white arrows up, rows,
rows — face with helmet — fires of
shadows resounding, tree & figure
golden pipes, fire & cow, single flame

9 7 05

blue between cliff & building

lights of cars, flashlights in the
snow, lines crackling out
long gray guns in the dark blue
green nest under chair

tires, ringed in white light, on old
buicks with running boards
a muddy river beyond the town
each morning, at 4, someone runs past

the light is like an arrow into the sky
pulling up to find
rocks to go to the bottom of the blue
to rest & build

a corridor of golden figures, buildings
winged figure, light green, flies in
robe with golden light creases
figures in tan robes stand in a line

move upside down through the water
circular movement with opening at center
covered wagons up a hill, blue sky
broom, wheel, pants, path, dress, elk

small boat barely misses ship
face, with light on forehead, like a
harbor — light across the river like
a keyboard, wheel, with golden

wings & dark eyes, glides down
golden wings lift, spray light down
half circle of yellow & pink horizon
light blue wings pull giant tree

wasps out of golden rings
giant, thin, sky blue wings — insect
with great black eyes, thin body
underwater golden sashes unfurl

scarlet lines, thick, curl & bring up
a water rush of long-stemmed white
flowers — water falls down on
white bird flying, flower with round

diamond in its upper opening, lavender
walls against darkness, winged fish
fish small & large in healthy blue water
hand turns & is reflected in water, golden
arm, golden fish, circle of light, golden trail

9 8 05

Golden Leaves Across The Emerald

leaves, golden, into the sky

the winds have blown past
the leaves filled the air like
hummingbird wings
white rockets have filled the sky

& now man is sleeping
candles lit, the cats are in
water buffalo enter the door
one by one, water creates a blue

river full of knives
be altogether a hand between con-
verging rivers — outside an orange
building, a crowd of men

hope, bed, death, love of dark, friend-
ship — blue waters with arc of
light surrendering
water shines down as it pushes forward

hope indeed — a guitar & teeth
arrow through the star
orange skiff into blue, fish & cat
the long, pointed leaves grow upward

& bend, carry & hold, stare straight
are always carried into lavender skies
a mouth, like citizen kane, like stalin,
opens, murmurs — dark orange & gold

bands above the horizon, beyond the
house — house with two owls
gray & mint green, bright red around
the golden center — white teeth & candle

a man dances in a spotlight
the long line of blackbirds divide
light from dark — light sprays forth
like a train moving across nebraska

brakeman, church pews, snow around
the old man's face — breath, fall
love circles back around the cows
nothing lost, the trees covered with snow

blue feathers form half a circle
gold banks, blue water with red wood
a clearing & trees out of the gold — home,
bright, solace, gold & blue & cow's skull

9 11 05

arrow up into light with wings

golden sails, blue boats, diamonds
wreath of blueberries, house
yellow diamond eyes, purple evening
he said 5 syllables, 7 syllables, 5

syllables was the perfect haiku
the u.s. has a yellow, vibrating perimeter
like a golden belt around his dress blues
single stalk of corn fronts the sun

columns of projected light — arms,
with feathers below, raised — confidence
& love — train across the prairie, smoke
billowing — a bonnet like golden wings

commemorates the downward splashing
light of an eagle, a ship, a rower, a
snow-capped mountain — arrows in their
hands — in the middle a hand opens up

white figure glides downward
ships across a lake, large dark wings
like a cloud & then the golden & black
plane dives & like an arrow, explodes

each time the green frog goes up
the fresh wood, water smoothes,
its surface has a mushroom-shaped
fire-glow — all white the arm & bow

of the hunter, a man on a horse,
black wall & spinning draws light
into darkness — wide wings above
the green figure gliding sideways

barrels of light at its inner walls
golden walls & gate, opens, magenta
flower the queen, an arrow shot
through an arm, twisting, circling

green-golden wings with black
arrowhead rise, peach half with seed
blue shadow white wings yellow light
the arm held as it rolls, upward golden

hair, body sweeps upward, wings
land on curving blue band — high
in the night — snow & trees — many
peaches cut in half — light up & curves
the seeds are the eyes of the arrows

9 13 05

butterfly wings at base of cow skull

a slanted street with parked cars
purple circle like a spinning yoyo
tennis raquet, tree, quiet street
scissors, like a nude body, posed

feather, half-gold, half-white
fans in bleachers, looking up at a
spray of stars — turtle climbs up
belt of a man's & elk horns

golden-winged-bat flies down
fire among bricks — golden cow skull
long beak, feathers, arms — baseball
bat beside the spinning ponds

light from front of cow skull
the light begins to form two
walls — revolver — men push up wall
men sit by a lake, rain hits surface

blue sky deep, wings & light
plane like an arrow with tail fire
her mint green dress fills the sky
like a ship with silver masts, road

with golden arrow on the carrier's
surface — white chorus girls surround
the deep, high surf — yellow flowers
bloom, sun shines down in sheets

half moon, horizontal, bands of gold
across the sky — a shoe & a jet of light
road to left & road upward, golden cross,
like a knife, in between, quiet

before golden indian headdress, half
sun with lines outward from the
bison on the cave's wall, flames from
candles, a single, large eye surrounded

by jade in the dark — white fish with
white lines outward — armor — wings
upward from body, gravity, slender, hope,
half moon & half moon merge, shoe, wings

golden cow skull flies, tail of fire
above long narrow descent, white
feather on bended stem, juice, complete
sky of silver knives, golden & black lines
knives, arrows rushing between blood wings

9 15 05

golden fire trail diverges

river, white flowers, jets
space station twirls slowly
sunny day & a man walks past
a large green animal with white eyes

showers, lights, triangles of people
washing their foreheads & bellies
golden, wide-eared cat, like a bat
she draws out the situation & then

puts an absurd statement like death
when birth or love demand consecutive
images, laughter & kindness — they
were the reason he stayed at the

table — elk's horns higher than the
rockies — the white profile had a
chasm of golden light & the top of
the skull torn at the top, pulled

apart, dismantled, no chance of
reaching the other side — her body
shaped like gold fire — white wing
fallen, covered wagon continues

& the ring of wagons & the ring of fire
turns, tilts sideways in the night sky
vertically, horizontally, till leaves
appear & the beast sleeps, clean & safe

a green column twirls, with prayer
figure appearing at top & splashes of
light fall down — ships' artillery fire
the top of the room circles inward as

one eye, like sunflower fringes of the sun,
burn faster blue till white stem emerges
an angel with green eyes & wild hair
like splashing fire — moon far, full &

collected, like a crazy key & sparks on a
blue prairie night — peach cut open
green clothed figure with yellow hands
turns — a silver ship, leaves, yellow

flowers, dark smoke — a long black path
above the wheat field — white-robed figure
with arms up, triangles of light down
light, larger than a gun, road, fire, circular
blue, candlelight, rest, golden teeth, bridge

9 16 05

white pages black spine

full white moon seen through the
bedroom window at 4 a.m.

white rose, full, large, slowly turns
like a propeller, two white roses
dance in the darkness

white rose has dignity, turns, petals
fall, now slender as fred astaire
white diamond faraway in the night
sky

plates stacked sideways
a white rose stands in front, leans
against
vanilla ice cream cone, bugle, star-
shaped
man in black suit, white shirt
chair, water shimmering underneath
chinese man's face breaks in half
land of golden grain — white ship
moves across

jet trails upward like the sun shines
down, first silver-blue trail then fire
door falls, fire across the floor
into the quiet blue vase

white rose held upward with a single
flame at its center
the golden flame leads its way across
the sky
white circle, white spots, white
lines
long golden path with square end
eye (seductive) with golden path
straight down
fellowship, heart, love, kindness

two yellow-gold paths upward at
angles to roundness

cherish white & black & stairs
baby with golden wrappings
silver-white rings round
flame held by black arm surrounded by
purple blooms — morning breaks like a
mouth, golden shells, golden robe & fire
sun across horizon, white bone

9 17 05

white-winged figure above

white half circles & a white air
balloon — bone — arrows down like
tears, orange-handled scissors
sharp, sparkling knife — rush down-

ward of white jet fuel exhaust
like a dress — two white bottles,
two knives touch at tips — golden-
white fish swim among gold & black

bands across the width, fox eyes in
an owl's head, curious & mad, a nest
for light — fire like a shell, wings
jade head, paper plane flies into

profile, two hands go up each side of
eye as if to pray & lift, like surface
mist on faraway planet, yellow flowers
sprout in a long chorus line

wings thunder down against the
blue — regal, home, safe, warm, clean
the sacred text furled, carried under
one arm as wheels turn beside

eyes, like propellers, wait for the
downfall plunge — sparkling diamonds
on the ocean — night & a green-shaded
light shines down on a band of men

on a mountainside — city like a tree
arises, an aura around it — golden leaves
its perimeter, a purple ball its center
yellow leaves around the king on a red

carpet — yellow leaves with red lines down
the center, the flowers open like mouths
& a white path goes upward brushing blue-
ness to the sides — lights & blindfolds

white surface like an aircraft carrier
large red wasps, slingshots & trapeze
swinging in rain, twisting, circling, arrows
shot, from all angles, into the body, body

circles & held, dark house at center with
highways emerging, sword picked up
white flame center, gold lines, white bird
water breaks up, center bare, white horse
earth breaks from vase, fire line in blue

9 18 05

single nest at center end

golden nest with eggs, golden
lines & musical notes — a long
swan's neck & head bends over
the eggs — a horn like a flower

light path shoots diagonally upward
faraway golden star sparkles
white masks, musical notes like
sea horses, jubilant, bells ring

golden rings in the middle of a
meadow, pushed up above the smoke
golden fish — the morning's mint
green sky — golden flames, white

masks, green trees seen through the
windshield — narrow, high, blue water-
falls, at top a golden square — the
sound of someone trying to enter

beautiful white nude woman's body
curved white gold bending circling
narrow white long-stemmed flowers
upward, chairs & flames like beds

one single full secret bloom & face
half seen, diamond, waters hitting
shore, glittering lights ocean outward
moon & blue along the rocks, single

rose with weed within circling upward
with rose emerging above from its center
twisting & relaxing like a sombrero
above the blue mist waters, quiet

with a star sparkle far out
arrows, like forks, aslant against the
wall — horns, sticks beat a long, rust-
colored, hollowed-out tree — golden light

hits back of rose & petals near the light
fold inward — blue-green waters go up-
ward like a wall, golden waters curl
& form long tunnels — flowers trumpet

downward, golden circles like nests, golden
paths, many, downward, scythes & arms
golden paths upward to purple dark figure
eye, wings above, golden, stairs down, golden
heart opened, seed like blood, fire around

9 19 05

breasts like leaves

the pages in a book are like stones
in a river
cold, bright, flower-like
fire like a halo
atop a mountain

journey, circle, youth, white flowers
like jets, arrows
fire springs up like a flower bloom

alone, anxious, remembrance
rolling, gold unspooling
twisting turning running
suddenly a lake

halo of love, halo around her bosom
white flowers, cello & crescent fire
circles, animals toward polar horizons

quiet hand horizontal
cougar's head into window where wings
suddenly quivers of fire
alternate among the evening throat

a skip rope of time
white sheets on a line at evening
the constant jet fuel exhausts
bright skies above audiences

white wings fill the sky
source deep & bright, one figure
looks outward — mother gathering
what has dried, what never remains

golden roses at the feathered ends
of arrows in a quiver
the immense red in the dark sky
promise, cow's skull, wings

peaches cut in half, white crosses
her loins, a river, flower, valley

a word in reverse, tree, figure
in the dark rain, fire up with golden

center, a length with white wings
above — wings & the constant up going
fire path — trees uprooted, swirling
circles & mounds of light, time no
longer an abstract, white wings & sun

9 25 05

light behind the mask

the golden balls are whirling
around the world
a gold necklace around her neck
the cat's one eye with a gold sun

under it
a front cover of a book with a gold
square on it
an umbrella of gold under

a golden bowler hat
tuba, front of awning also
man reads letter, sees the hat
rain falls outside the back window

of a taxi
dark inside, a golden bowler
beside the dark figure
shining light, like the sun,

in front of the taxi's lights
bamboo wall beside rushing waters
figures standing, one has a yellow
scarf tied round his lower leg

a stamp of yellow, on the back
of his hand, like a leaf
a long, rolled-up whiteness moves
through the subway cars

a black & white sheet, rolled up,
tied at intervals, used to escape
pale blue, gold eyes, like a man
on skis, ropes around the shoes

foot on snow, a fiery gold races
around the tracks, through tunnels
a white sailboat glides to its dock
dark blue night, cat with white

fish in its mouth — a pale blue ship
high in the night sky follows a
hand playing red keys that set red
circles to vibrate & a small white

clock rings next to an opened heart
red hand, white reaching backward
a golden spoon pours golden liquid
white pages of a book, white clock
green leaves from dark eye, golden body

9 26 05

red-leaved road into the dark

the moon shaped like 3 ripe bananas
in a row, eyes like yellow wings
her hand at her throat
the blue cuts in half the gold

morning wraps around her face
leaving only her eye visible
a red necklace & a gold heart
the two women talk like rings

of gold — cars with their lights on
pass in opposite directions, laughter &
listening & the necklace, the white
collar won't go away — love songs

are whispered — a little girl like
wheat on the prairie, hears of her
mother's death & hurries home
red & gold tops of trees fill the heart

& move up the mountain — the jade
eye has a lavender path, like a
rothko stroke, above it — the eye,
once again, has air force wings

two women laugh — you are not
going to play again — the language
is like a speeded-up record
two hands & arms, demure pink,

from opposite directions come to meet
the blue globe, had a grid of red
around it & the road up & around
the hill was green — a far off light

a tree with white atop its green
slants — the green sides almost
touch the burning center
the eye, now large, gold interior

with red perimeter, death, birth,
song, mother, daughter — she waits,
her legs spread, & the moon shines
brightly, a horse with golden horns

appears, the dark young woman opens
the door & disappears — a ship with
golden sails transforms into a bird
its wings white, high above the red leaves

9 27 05

Harry E. Northup has had eight previous books of poetry published: *Amarillo Born* (Victor Jiminez Press, 1966); *the jon voight poems* (Mt. Alveno Press, 1973); *Eros Ash* (Momentum Press, 1976); *Enough The Great Running Chapel* (Momentum Press, 1982); *the images we possess kill the capturing* (the jesse press, 1988); *The Ragged Vertical* (Cahuenga Press, 1996); *Reunions* (Cahuenga Press, 2001); and *Greatest Hits, 1966–2001* (Pudding House Press, 2002).

Harry received his B.A. in English from California State University, Northridge, where he studied verse with Ann Stanford.

New Alliance Records has released his "Personal Crime," new & selected poems from 1966–1991, on CD & cassette audio recording, & "Homes" on CD, both produced by Harvey R. Kuberink.

Northup has made a living as an actor for thirty years, acting in thirty-seven films, including "Mean Streets," "Alice Doesn't Live Here Anymore," "Taxi Driver" (1976 Palme d'Or winner at Cannes), "Fighting Mad" (starring role), "Citizens Band," "Blue Collar," "Over the Edge" (starring role), "Tom Horn," "Used Cars," "Kansas," "The Silence of the Lambs" (1991 Oscar winner for Best Picture), "Philadelphia," "Bad Girls," "Beloved," and a remake of "The Manchurian Candidate."

Harry Northup has acted in forty-three television shows, including "E.R.," (guest star), "The Court" (recurring role), "In Cold Blood," (CBS mini-series), "The Deliberate Stranger," "The Day the Bubble Burst," and "Knots Landing" (recurring role).

Harry has been a member of the Academy of Motion Picture Arts & Sciences since 1976.

He lives in Los Angeles with his wife, Holly Prado Northup.

Also Available from Cahuenga Press

Jonathan Cott
Homelands, 2000 (978-0-9649240-7-9; 69 pp; $12.00)

James Cushing
You and the Night and the Music, 1991 (OP; 86 pp)
The Length of an Afternoon, 1999 (978-0-09649240-6-2; 91 pp.; $12.00)
Undercurrent Blues, 2005 (978-0-9715519-4-7; 114 pp; $15.00)

Phoebe MacAdams
Ordinary Snake Dance, 1994 (62 pp; $10.00)
Livelihood, 2003 (978-0-9715519-1-6; 94 pp; $12.00)

Harry E. Northup
The Ragged Vertical, 1996 (978-0-9649240-0-0; 262 pp; $15.00)
Reunions, 2001 (978-0-9649240-9-3; 255 pp; $15.00)

Holly Prado
Specific Mysteries, 1990 (OP; 55 pp)
Esperanza: Poems for Orpheus, 1998 (978-0-9649240-5-5; 83 pp; $12.00)
These Mirrors Prove It: Selected Poems and Prose, 1970–2003, 2004 (978-0-9715519-3-0; 429 pp; $20.00)

Ann Stanford
Dreaming the Garden, 2000 (978-0-9649240-8-6; 77 pp; $15.00)

Cecilia Woloch
Sacrifice, 1997 (978-0-9649240-4-8; 95 pp; $12.00)
Tsigan, 2002 (978-0-9715519-0-9; 82 pp; $13.00)

Please add $5.50 per order for tax/shipping/handling. Order by mail or through our website:

Cahuenga Press
1256 N. Mariposa Avenue
Los Angeles, CA 90029

www.cahuengapress.com